D1488579

Teaching Beginning Reading and Writing

WITH THE PICTURE WORD INDUCTIVE MODEL

Emily F. Calhoun

ASCD

Association for Supervision and Curriculum Development
Alexandria, Virginia   USA

Association for Supervision and Curriculum Development
1703 N. Beauregard St. • Alexandria, VA 22311-1714 USA
Telephone: 1-800-933-2723 or 703-578-9600 • Fax: 703-575-5400
Web site: http://www.ascd.org • E-mail: member@ascd.org
Author guidelines: www.ascd.org/write

Printed in the United States of America.

S3/99

ISBN-13: 978-0-87120-337-3
ASCD Stock No. 199025

Library of Congress Cataloging-in-Publication Data
Calhoun, Emily.
   Teaching beginning reading and writing with the picture word
inductive model / Emily F. Calhoun.
     p. cm.
   Includes bibliographical references.
   ISBN 0-87120-337-5
   1. Language arts (Primary) 2. Reading (Primary) 3.
Reading—Phonetic method. 4. English language—Composition and
exercises—Study and teaching (Primary) 5. Pictures in education.
I. Title.
   LB1528 .C35 1999
   372.6—dc21   98-58153
                                                     CIP

11 10 09 08 07   10 9 8 7 6 5 4 3

What teachers do

in the structuring of learning opportunities

and the provision of instruction

is at the heart of the contribution schools make

to the academic achievement of students.

Hawley, Rosenholtz, Goodstein, and Hasselbring, 1984

Teaching Beginning Reading and Writing with the Picture Word Inductive Model

You can read the chapters in the order presented; however, if you read the Preface and chapters 1 and 2, you may choose to jump into Chapter 5 and begin using the model. Then, as you practice, use the other chapters to help you move forward with learning the model.

Preface

This book is about teaching beginning reading and writing. It is based on the belief that we can teach children to be more observant and conscious of the patterns at work as people communicate—particularly through reading and writing—and that as teachers we can use what they are able to do and what they are able to see to bring them rapidly and naturally into greater literacy.

As author, I have three primary objectives: (1) to share the picture word inductive model (PWIM) for teaching beginning reading and writing; (2) to encourage the writing and reading of informative prose with beginning readers; and (3) to promote continuous focused inquiry into the development of literacy and into the results of teacher-and-student interactions.

Objective one is specific and limited to introducing and explaining the picture word inductive model. The PWIM is a strategy that uses an integrated language arts approach to teaching beginning reading and writing, and it includes the component skills of phonetic analysis, structural analysis, spelling, and mechanics.

Objective two is simple but potentially far-reaching: Increased attention to writing and reading informative prose could improve the quality of students' writing and their comprehension of informative and expository prose. In most classrooms and schools, we do much more with fiction and narrative writing and reading in our primary curriculum than we do with nonfiction and the development of informative, high-quality prose. The PWIM can help us to provide a better curricular and instructional balance by focusing lessons on composing and comprehending nonfiction prose.

Objective three is general and complex and includes illustrating a teaching stance that analyzes how language works, teaches students to engage in a parallel analysis, analyzes students' responses to instructional moves, and takes action based on these responses. This teaching stance has allowed me to continue learning about reading, writing, and teaching for more than a quarter century, and I'm not finished yet!

I am passionate about the PWIM, but I feel the same way about other teaching strategies that are flexible, comprehensive, fun, and productive for students. I've used the PWIM since 1976—longer than most other strategies—as a 1st grade teacher and later with students ranging from kindergarten, to middle school, to adult nonreaders. During the last 20 years, I have taught many kindergarten, 1st grade, 2nd grade, upper-elementary and special-needs teachers to use the model as a vehicle for integrating language arts. I've watched their success and delight with students' growth in reading and writing. Working with others has given me many opportunities to learn from them and from their applications of the model, and has pushed me toward greater clarity in articulating the sequence and rationale for the model.

What would you see if you visited some of these teachers? If you visited one classroom over several days and watched the teacher use the picture word inductive model, you would see students generating words and sentences about a large picture and studying those words and sentences. Some days a lesson would last 15 minutes, other days 35 minutes. The students would be working in various ways depending on the task: individual students classifying the words; pairs of students reading sentences to each other; all the students working with the teacher on one useful phonics generalization; or individuals or large groups writing a paragraph about the picture and thinking about a title that accurately describes the picture. For the casual observer, the lessons might seem simplistic; the knowledgeable observer might become excited about the number, range, and complexity of language concepts being taught.

If you visited several classrooms, you would see some teachers using picture word lessons for a small portion of their daily language arts instruction. You would see other teachers using the lessons of the picture word inductive model as a framework for language arts units, thus their lessons consume a larger portion of the instructional day. You would notice that some teachers limit the use of the model to building sight vocabulary and the recognition and use of phonics and spelling patterns, while other teachers extend its use as far into the communications process as the students are able to participate—for example, into modeling and providing students practice with sentence and paragraph construction.

If you observed a few teachers for several weeks, you would discover that the lesson structure of the picture word inductive model keeps students engaged in continuous inquiry into how language works and keeps teachers engaged in continuous inquiry into how students are progressing as readers and writers. Thus, along with promoting student growth in reading and writing, long-term use of the model teaches students how to learn about language and helps teachers learn how to study student progress in reading and writing.

▼   ▼   ▼

Using the printed page, I'll take you into a few classrooms to see what inquiring minds can find. As you read the scenarios of teachers and students using the model, I hope you will feel its potential uses. As you read the sections on rationale and theoretical underpinnings, I hope you will form hypotheses about the different moves or sequences that compose the model and test them in your own classroom. And, of course, my personal teacher's dream is that something here will support student growth in reading and writing and your continued inquiry into language literacy.

EMILY F. CALHOUN

1

Glimpsing the Model
in Kindergarten and 2nd Grade

In this five-day scenario, about six weeks into the school year, we visit with Nancy Tayloe and her kindergarten students as they use the picture word inductive model. Ms. Tayloe's 5-year-old students at Ben Hill Elementary School are working on building their reading vocabularies. They are also beginning their study of phonics by analyzing the structures of words that are in their listening, speaking, and reading vocabularies. Later in the chapter we'll visit a 2nd grade classroom for three weeks of lessons.

The children are seated on the floor, facing a poster that features a teddy bear propped against a tree in a large yard or park. The poster is mounted in the middle of a large blank sheet of paper. Ms. Tayloe says, "We're going to get some of the words for this week's reading vocabulary by shaking words out of this picture. I want you to study the picture carefully and when I call on you, come up and point to something in the picture and say what it is. Then I'll write the word and draw a line from that part of the picture to the word. We'll start learning to read the words as we go along."

The children study the picture (Figure 1.1). After a few minutes, Ms. Tayloe asks them if they have found something they'd like to share. All hands go up, and Ms. Tayloe calls on Celeste.

Celeste reaches up, points, and says, "That's a *ladder*."

Ms. Tayloe draws a line from the ladder and writes *ladder* in large print, announcing each letter as she writes it: "l-a-d-d-e-r spells *ladder*." She then spells *ladder* again, while the children watch and listen. "Now, I'll spell it again, and you say each letter after me." She does, and then asks another child for a word.

"Small ladder," says Brent. "There's another ladder, a *small ladder*."

Ms. Tayloe draws a line from the small ladder and writes *small ladder* in large print, announcing each letter as she writes it: "s-m-a-l-l spells *small*; *ladder*, l-a-d-d-e-r spells *ladder*. *Small ladder*," she says as she places her hand under the first word and then the next. Then she asks the students to spell the words with her.

"Sit," says Marvin, and points to the teddy bear. "The bear's *sitting*."

Ms. Tayloe draws a line from the bear's seat and writes *sitting*. She spells the word aloud and then asks the children to spell the word with her.

She then points to the first word. "What is this word?"

"*Ladder*," they chorus.

Ms. Tayloe asks, "And if you saw the word and couldn't remember it or weren't quite sure, what could you do?"

"Go down the line to the ladder in the picture," they say.

"Right," Ms. Tayloe responds. "Find the word or the group of words, trace the line, and check your reading."

The lesson continues. "And what's this word?" Ms Tayloe asks, pointing to the word *small*.

"Small," they chorus again. She repeats the process with *ladder* then asks for the whole phrase, and calls on Chris.

"*Small ladder*," says Chris.

"Who thinks she's right?" asks Ms. Tayloe. The children's hands go

Figure 1.1

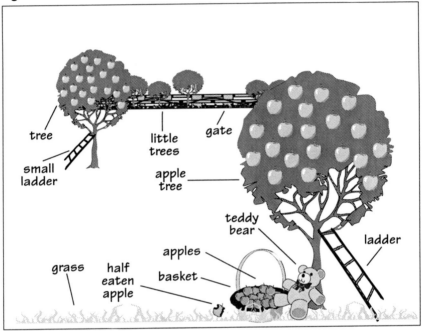

Select pictures that appeal to your students and that use their spoken vocabulary. Use a photograph to help build their observation and research skills.

up. The teacher continues to elicit words from the children, continuing the pattern as before, examining each word and regularly reviewing all of them.

By the end of the session the class has identified the words listed in Figure 1.2 (p. 4) and can say each word as the teacher points to it and runs her hand down the line for them to check their reading. Ms. Tayloe finishes this segment of the picture word inductive model by asking the students to notice if any of the same words appear in the books they are taking home for the evening to share with their parents.

The following day, as the children enter the classroom, some go to the picture word chart and look at the words, saying them to each other and following the lines from the words they don't remember to the elements of the picture. Again, the children sit near the poster. Ms. Tayloe has them read the words, using the picture to help them locate the referents for the words.

Ms. Tayloe has taken the computer file of words that were shaken out of the picture and printed them in large type to make word cards. She includes duplicates of the words that were listed more than once—such as two ladders and two baskets. Ms. Tayloe gives each child a complete set of word cards and asks them to read their set. If they can't remember a word, they are expected to go to the poster, match the word, and trace the line to the part of the picture it represents.

Figure 1.2

ladder	apple with a leaf
sitting	tree trunk
bear's	little trees
apples	half-eaten apple
teddy bear	bear
apple	apple
tree	core
basket	leaf
grass	trunk
tree	teddy
tree	apple
basket	little
apple core	half-eaten
gate	trees
ladder	

Much activity ensues. The children find their personal space, spread out their word cards, peer at the words, and say them (usually aloud) to themselves. Occasionally, the students ask Ms. Tayloe if they are right, and she sends them to the picture to find out for themselves. Soon, children are getting up and down, holding a word card and locating the word on the chart.

As she moves around the classroom, Ms. Tayloe encourages the students, notes which students are reading their words correctly, which words are causing the most difficulty, and which students need to visit and revisit the chart.

She notices that Derrick has his word card with *apple* upside down as he searches the chart. She takes his card and turns it right-side-up, saying, "Try it this way, Derrick. Some of these letters are tricky and you have to study them very carefully." She notices Janine is getting frustrated as she searches for *half-eaten* and gives her a clue by saying, "Janine, this word describes one of the apples; take a look at the bottom of the chart."

After 30 minutes, most of the students are still actively engaged with studying and reading their words, but Ms. Tayloe decides this is enough for today's lesson. "All right, let's put our word cards back in their envelopes."

The following morning, she again reviews the chart with the children. Then she asks them to take out their word cards and put words together according to how they are spelled. Ricardo says that *tree* and *trees* and *ladder* have two letters just alike. Ms. Tayloe asks him to point to the letters and he does. Jan put *apple* and *teddy* together because one has two *p*'s together and the other has two *d*'s together. Kareem responds to Jan's category by saying that *apples* has two just alike; Brian put *teddy* and *ladder* together because they have two *d*'s in the middle.

Ms. Tayloe decides to expand on that point by asking the students to look at *apple* and *apples* and to figure out how the words are the same and how they are different. Robin responds by saying that they are spelled the same except for the circles on the end. After prompting, Robin says that *apples* has the circles on the end, and Zoe says *s*, apples has an *s*. And *apple* is just one apple and *apples* is two apples.

The students continue sharing their categories. Ms. Tayloe pauses when *tree* and *trunk* are placed together because of the *tr* at the beginning. She asks, "Now, think very carefully." She takes a pair of scissors and cuts a bit off one edge. "I just trimmed this piece of paper. How do you think the word *trim* will be spelled at the beginning?"

The children are puzzled for a minute, and then hands begin to go up. Ms. Tayloe waits until nearly all the pupils have an idea, and then calls on Bernardo, "Like *tree*!"

The class discusses Bernardo's answer, and then Ms. Tayloe writes *trim* on a blank poster near the chart. They all read the set of words on the chart once more, and end for the day. Ms. Tayloe finishes by asking the children to see if they notice any words that begin like *tree*, *trunk*, and *trim* in the books they are taking home for the evening to share with their parents. If they find any new words she says they should write them down to add to the new poster tomorrow.

On the fourth day, after they have read the words on the chart, Ms. Tayloe and her students develop sentences about the picture. The sentences include "The teddy bear is sitting in the countryside," and "There are apples all over the place." One child points to an apple core and wonders, "Who do you suppose ate that apple? Can teddy bears eat apples?" Ms. Tayloe records about a dozen sentences, and they read them together before closing the session.

The next morning, every student receives a printout of the previous day's sentences including the author's name. Their task is to find a word they can read, find their own sentence, and just have fun reading what they have created.

In this scenario, Ms. Tayloe was using the picture word inductive *Summary* model to elicit words from the children's listening and speaking vocabularies. She then helped the students to study and begin to master those words for use in their individual reading and writing. By reclassifying some of the words according to letter sounds, she also began an early exploration of phonics.

The PWIM in 2nd Grade

We drop in on Ms. Frazier and her 2nd grade combination class the third week of school. Ms. Frazier has 22 students, 10 native English speakers and 12 students whose native language is Spanish. These 12 students entered kindergarten with limited English proficiency and were in a transitional bilingual program during kindergarten and 1st grade. Ms. Frazier speaks a little Spanish but is not fluent; however, she is familiar with second language development. This is the second unit in which students have used the picture word inductive model and Ms.

Frazier is still teaching them the moves of the model.

Ms. Frazier gathers the students in front of a large picture that is stapled to the bulletin board and centered in the middle of two large strips of light-blue board paper. As they seat themselves on the rug, she says, "Make sure you have your personal space around you and that you can see the picture." She takes a minute to help students adjust their spaces and continues, "We're going to work with this picture for the next few days, just like we did with the picture of the playground. We'll shake a lot of words out, learn to read and spell those words, and maybe we'll write about the picture so we can practice our writing. Now, be ready to tell us something you recognize in the picture. Everybody will have a chance to share."

Ms. Frazier waits about a minute until most hands are up and calls on Enrique, "What's something you see in this picture?"

Enrique points to a necktie one of the children in the picture is wearing and says, "That's a *necktie*."

Ms. Frazier draws a line from the necktie to the paper and says "*Necktie*. Now, I want you to listen while I spell *necktie* first and then we'll spell it together so that you get lots of practice on your spelling." The children listen while Ms. Frazier says, "N-e-c-k-t-i-e," and writes the letters as she says them. Then again, "N-e-c-k-t-i-e spells *necktie*. Now, all together."

The children chorus the spelling as Ms. Frazier points to each letter. "Now, that spells . . . ?"

"*Necktie!*"

Ms. Frazier calls on Maryanne, who points to a roll of tape in the picture and says, "*Tape*."

Ms. Frazier draws a line from the roll of tape to the paper and says, "Now, let's learn how to spell *tape*." She spells it, then has the students spell it as she points to each letter and says "Now, t-a-p-e spells . . .?"

"*Tape*," the children say almost in unison.

For the next 20 minutes, the group continues to shake words out of the picture. *Gold letters, books, white board,* and *children* are quickly identified. For each word, Ms. Frazier spells the word and pronounces it again, and then the children spell and pronounce it. One student adds *people* as another word for the group of children in the picture.

Periodically, Ms. Frazier reviews the words, pointing to each and showing the students how they can follow the line from the word to the object it refers to. As in their first unit, they are building a picture dictionary. If they need the meaning of a word for independent reading or writing, they can trace the line from the word to the object.

Yellow book and *blue book* and *shiny book* are added to the chart. *T-shirt* is volunteered and Ms. Frazier spells it t-e-e s-h-i-r-t. Harry bursts out with, "That's not *T-shirt*. It's spelled with a big T!" Ms. Frazier adds *T-shirt* to the chart as well. She has students read both versions but spell only *shirt* with her. She says, "I'll have to check and see if both spellings are correct. See what you can find out." *Boy, girl, uniform,* and *uniforms* are added, as are *green hat* and *picture.* Altogether, about 25 words appear.

Ms. Frazier reviews all the words with the children, then leads them into a discussion of the picture: "Now, several of you asked me where these children are. Where do you think they are?"

"School," says Marta.

"How many of you agree with Marta? And what makes you think they are in school?"

"Well, it could be a family, but there are too many children."

One student asks, "Why are they all wearing red?" Ms. Frazier has them speculate for a while and ideas like "special class" and "their school makes them do it" surface.

Robert suggests that it's probably a school because there's a white board in the picture and most houses don't have white boards. Francesca suggests that the presence of a big library corner makes it likely that the picture is of a group of students at school.

Paul says it can't be a home because there are too many books.

Anna adds, "And homes don't have bookcases." There's some discussion about these statements.

Finally, Ms. Frazier confirms that it is a school. In this school students wear uniforms; the school is in Nottingham, England, about 6,500 miles from their school in California; and these are 5-year-old students. Ms. Frazier shows the class a map and asks Sarah to come up and put her hand on California. Ms. Frazier puts her hand on Nottingham to show the distance.

"Tomorrow we'll continue with our picture. When you have a little time today, practice reading our words. If you have trouble reading a word, what do you do?" asks Ms. Frazier.

"Trace the line to the picture," says the class.

And the first lesson ends.

The next day the students gather around the picture at 9 a.m. and Ms. Frazier announces, "We're going to work on our silent reading a little before we read our new words."

Ms. Frazier points to *book* on the picture chart. "*Book!*" she shouts. "Was I reading that word silently?"

"Noooo," they respond.

"That's right. I read it aloud, didn't I? Now, as we read the words around the picture, I'll point to a word, and you say it silently to yourself. Then I'll trace the line from the word to the picture so we can check our reading, and then we'll say the word silently and then read and spell it together, aloud. Let's do one together for practice. Here we go, silently."

Ms. Frazier points to a word and about half the children read it aloud. She says, "Let's all read it again . . . silently. Don't let any letter sounds or words escape your mouth. Here we go, just practice reading it in your mind." She points to a word, holding her hand against her lips, everyone is silent. She traces the line, "Now, aloud."

"*Boy*," they chorus.

"Great!" exclaims Ms. Frazier. "Look at this word. Read it silently. Don't let any words or any letter sounds escape from your mouth." She points to *uniforms* and traces one line and then the other to students wearing uniforms, and then says, "Now, aloud."

"*Uniforms*," they chorus.

"What good readers. Let's do another one." And the process continues, with Ms. Frazier pointing to words, the students reading them silently, Ms. Frazier tracing the line so they can check their reading, and everyone reading the words aloud.

Ms. Frazier gives them envelopes with word cards from yesterday's work and says, "For the next 15 minutes, I want everyone to work individually on reading your set of words. Use the picture chart when you need to."

They begin the third lesson the next morning with a quick review of the chart. After all the words are read, Ms. Frazier begins to prepare students for the process of classification. She begins with concrete objects because the attributes are so easily clarified.

Ms. Frazier picks up a yellow plastic bucket and shakes it, "What's this?" The class responds:

- Our math bucket;
- Our pattern blocks;
- Our shapes; and
- Triangles and rectangles.

Ms. Frazier says, "I'm going to select some pattern blocks from this bucket. I'm going to sort out some and put them together. I want you to think about why I put them together. See if you can come up with at least two reasons."

Ms. Frazier pulls out five pattern blocks and holds them so students can see them. Then she calls on Kerri, who says, "You put them together because they're all red."

"How many of you agree with Kerri that these are all red?" Hands go up. "Does anyone have another reason?" Scott volunteers that they have four sides. Again, Ms. Frazier asks who agrees. They all do.

Serena says, "You put them together because they are red, have four sides, and are square."

"Serena just gave us three reasons why I might have put these pattern blocks together," says Ms. Frazier. "Who agrees with all three reasons?" Some students who saw only one attribute come to recognize that the teacher made a category of objects that have several attributes in common.

"Now, let's switch to words. I want you to learn to study words carefully and put them together in groups based on how they are spelled or what they mean." She places several word cards in the large pocket chart with the words turned away from the students. "I want you to do the same kind of detective work with these words as you just did with our pattern blocks," says Ms. Frazier as she turns the cards over. "Everyone read them silently." Then she demonstrates "checking your reading" by taking each card and placing it under the matching word on the chart and running her finger down the line to the object(s). Ms. Frazier has chosen the word cards *person*, *people*, and *pictures*.

"Now, why do you think I might have put these words together?" asks the teacher.

She calls on Jeselle, who shyly ventures that the reason is that all three words begin with *p*.

"Who agrees? These three words begin with the letter *p*?" Ms. Frazier pauses for the students to study the words for a few seconds. "Now," says Ms. Frazier, "let's read the words together and see if you can come up with another reason why I might have put them together." They read them, first silently, then aloud, as she points to them. "Now, I am going to read them aloud and you listen. See if you can think of another reason. You were right, one reason was they all begin with the letter *p* as in *pig*."

She pronounces *person*, *people*, and *pictures* carefully and several hands go up. She calls on Annelle who states that the words all have *e* in them, and *people* has two *e*'s.

"That's correct," says Ms. Frazier. "What else can you discover?"

"Person has a 'son' in it," observes Ron.

"Can you think of anything else, Christina?" asks Ms. Frazier.

Christina responds that it's like they're two words. Ms. Frazier prompts Christina to explain that, and the student says that it's like it has two parts, two pieces. The teacher then pronounces the three words, slightly emphasizing the two syllables. "Good thinking, you discovered both reasons I put those words together: They all begin with *p* and they all have two parts or syllables. Would *paper* fit in this group?" She writes *paper* on the board and the students assure her it would fit the group.

"How about *pen*?" asks Ms. Frazier. There is some disagreement about whether *pen* would belong, so Ms. Frazier uses the difference between *pen* and *pencil* for a little more practice. Then she asks the students to "sort the words in your envelope any way you want to, and be prepared to share your groups and tell us why you put the words together."

She passes out the envelopes, helps the students spread out, and they get to work. Ms. Frazier circulates, observing the word groups being formed, checking to be sure the students can read the words, sending some students to the chart to check their reading, and asking students to tell her why they put words together.

Lots of categories emerge (see Figure 1.3). Although many students have similar groups, what they see in the words and what they can articulate vary widely. Some students attend more to letters and sounds, some to the meanings of words, and some to a combination.

Ms. Frazier ends this lesson by commenting on several categories and then uses her large word cards to share the category containing *book*, *board*, and *boy*. The class discusses the initial /b/ sound and the varying sounds of /oo/, /oa/, and /oy/. Their homework is to find at least six words that begin with *b* and *o*, list them on a piece of paper, and drop them in the picture word box in the morning.

On Thursday, they begin with a quick review of the words and add a few words to the chart. Then Ms. Frazier uses some of the words from the homework papers for a short explicit-instruction lesson on /oo/, /oa/, and /oy/. Part of the content generated by students during this

Figure 1.3—Word Groups Categorized by Students

After using the PWIM to shake words out of a picture, the students practice grouping words into their own categories. Using the PWIM in this way gives students experience with early phonics and spelling.

Student-identified word categories	Students explain their word categories
book, boy, board	• All begin with *b* • All have the same two first letters
book, books, black, board, blue	• All begin with the letter *b* and have one part
picture, people, person	• All have *p*'s • All have *p*'s at the beginning • All have *p*'s as the first letter and two parts • All have *p*'s at the beginning and they all have *e*'s
girl, boy, child, children, people, person	• All humans • All are names for people when we don't know their names • All are people
black book, yellow book, blue book	• All have *book* • All have the color of the book • All have two *o*'s
green hat, black book, red T-shirt, yellow book, blue book, white board, gold letters	• All have color words
necktie, white board, child, children, shiny book, hair, red T-shirt, girls, pictures	• All have *i*'s
boy, girl, child, children	• All are names for kids

segment includes a list of words that rhyme with *book* and *boy* and a discussion of the influence of *r* on vowels. Then she asks students to reclassify their words to see if they can identify any new groups, and to make sure they can read every word on the chart. Their homework is to ~extens~ see if they can find any more words that stand for people when we don't know their names.

During Friday's lesson, Ms. Frazier begins working with the students on titles and sentences. She's worked with them a little on titles during read-aloud time and during their group language- experience lessons. As the students gather around the picture, she says, "Who remembers what a title does?" The responses include "Names of books," "Names of stories," "Covers of books," "Tells us what the story's about." Ms. Frazier asks the students to study the picture carefully and think of a good title for it. She gives them a minute to think, then collects about 10 titles. As students volunteer titles, she asks them how the various titles relate to the picture. Some are comprehensive and accurate; some are less so; and some are sentences. Here are a few of their responses:

"I think the picture should be called 'all colors,' because there are so many colors in it."

"'Children in uniforms,' 'cause they're all wearing red uniforms."

"'Shiny books,' there are lots of shiny books in their school."

"'Kids in school.' They are at school."

After listening to some proposed titles, Ms. Frazier notes to herself that she wants to bring a few books to class to spark discussion using both familiar titles and new ones; she'll talk with students about length, content, and promises to the reader represented by informative titles. For now, however, they move on to sentences.

Ms. Frazier writes *sentence* on the board and under it she writes two of the sentences she heard during discussion:

- The students are all wearing uniforms.
- There are young kids gathered around their teacher.

She asks the students to read the sentences silently, reading as many words as they can. Then they read the sentences together.

"Remember, we helped Davida turn the first sentence into the title Students Wearing Uniforms because Davida mentioned that the students are all wearing uniforms. That seemed really weird to her, and so much of the picture was taken up by students in uniforms. And Gini came up with the title of Children Around Their Teacher. Well, that is good thinking. You came up with some nice titles that describe what is happening or what we can see in our picture. Later, we'll work on titles again. For journal time, you may want to write something that goes with your title.

"Now, homework," says Ms. Frazier. "Study our picture sometime today and pretend you are going to write a letter describing the picture to someone who has not seen it. Be ready on Monday to share something from your pretend letter."

On Monday morning, when it's picture word time, Ms. Frazier has the overhead projector set up. She and the students begin the lesson with a quick reading of the picture word chart, work on two target sight words, and add a few more /oo/, /oa/, and /oy/ words to the wall charts. They spend the next two days generating and recording sentences describing things in the picture. The sentences cover almost everything in the picture. Of course, not all students generated complete sentences. For example, "Gold letters are on the uniform" began with a student observing "gold letters." The teacher prompted the student by asking where the letters appear. The teacher worked with the student's response of "On the uniform" to produce the sentence. Other sentences proposed by the students include the following:

- They like school because they're smiling.
- They like to read because they have books all around them.
- The tops of the uniforms are all alike, but the bottoms are different for boys and girls.

When the students offer ideas that are not obvious or that might require interpretation, Ms. Frazier asks them for their evidence. For example, the proposed sentence "The children are learning by listening to the teacher" prompted the teacher to ask, "Why do you say that?"

"They are all being quiet, sort of leaning close to the teacher, and it doesn't look like they're talking," responds the student.

Serena adds, "They are learning because they are good listeners and they read lots of books."

"All the kids in this picture love school."

"They look like they are happy."

"Why do you think so?" Ms. Frazier asks.

"Most of them are smiling. They look like they're happy working together."

"These kids are learning how to read and write."

"How do you know?" Ms. Frazier asks. "Could they be getting ready for music?"

"I see their work, and they have a chart up too! And you said they were kindergarten kids."

On Wednesday, the teachers gives each student a copy of all the sentences printed on light green paper. The next few lessons focus on learning to read the sentences. As Ms. Frazier walks around listening to the students read their sentences, she targets some high-frequency words (*in, on, The/the, They/they*) for additional work.

The following week students begin classifying the sentences. Ms. Frazier has them work with partners, and they spend several days reading and classifying sentences. At first, Ms. Frazier just observes and listens to their categories; she wants to find out how they are thinking and to be sure their reasons for grouping are accurate. About half the students put sentences together based on how they are written and what word starts the sentence (these all begin with *they*; these begin with *they are*).

One student describes her category as "all have five words and the word *the* in them." About half the students put sentences together based on a topic or what they think the sentences are about, such as students in uniforms or what's in the room. Some students group their sentences according to both content and sentence structure.

After the second session of reading sentences and classifying them however they wish, Ms. Frazier selects one of the topic categories she has noticed several students use. Ms. Frazier uses the category to demonstrate grouping sentences by content. She asks students to find a partner and encourages every partnership to find at least one group of sentences that go together because of what they are about. Before they begin, however, Ms. Frazier does a quick drill on *an*, *and*, *are*, *all*—high-frequency words that she's heard some students confuse and that she wants every student to master.

Through the PWIM, Ms. Frazier is preparing her students for work on writing informative paragraphs about a single topic and main idea, and is showing them how an accurate brief description of their category can provide a good title. For their next lesson, Ms. Frazier will take one of their categories, put together a paragraph, and then talk about how she formed the paragraph.

On Thursday, Ms. Frazier begins the picture word lesson by telling the students that they've put together a number of good categories with their sentences. She elaborates, "Some of you put together sentences about uniforms; some about all the colors in the picture; some about the books, where they were and how they were being used; and some about what the students were doing. Several of you put together three or four different categories, and some of you have written your own piece about what you were most interested in.

"Well, I took one of your categories," says Ms. Frazier as she places five of their sentences in a large pocket chart, "and I wrote a paragraph about our picture. Let's read these sentences, then I'll share my para-graph." Ms. Frazier chose the following sentences:

- They have many talents.
- They are learning how to write words and spell.
- They are learning by listening to the teacher and by reading lots of books.
- They look like they are happy working together.
- All the kids in this picture love school.

Ms. Frazier continues, "There are lots of good groups we could write about, but I selected this one because when I asked why you put them together, you talked about kids learning. And that's one of the things I think is special when I look at our picture, and that's what I wanted to write about."

Ms. Frazier displays this title and paragraph on the overhead projector:

All Kids Learning

These young students have many talents. They're learning how to write words and how to spell. Reading lots of books and listening to the teacher helps them learn. They look like they're happy working together. The kids in this classroom love school because they are learning.

Ms. Frazier gives students time to read the paragraph silently, then she reads it aloud and briefly talks about how to tell the reader *who* (young students), *what* (learning happily), *how* (by reading lots of books, by listening to the teacher, by working together, and because they have many talents) and *where* (in a classroom).

Ms. Frazier continues by explaining why she changed the first *They* to *These young students*, why she added the second *how to* in the second sentence, and why she replaced *picture* with *classroom* in the last sentence. Ms. Frazier puts her first draft on the projector as she talks about a couple of the changes she made in word order and sentence order, and students ask her about a few of the changes from the original sentences.

One student suggests the last sentence needs to be the first sentence. Ms. Frazier agrees that it would make a good opening sentence and that they could switch the first and last sentence and the paragraph would still have the same main message. She also shares why she decided to open with the sentence about talents: "When I look at the picture it reminds me a bit of looking at you and how I feel about you as learners. I have a room full of smart and talented students who can learn anything they want to."

One student suggests that she add "in Nottingham, England," to the first sentence.

"That's good thinking, Enrique," says Ms. Frazier, "because that would tell the reader more about who and where. But where they are attending school wasn't so important to what I wanted to say in my paragraph. Now, if I had been writing about uniforms, I might . . ."

We have been visiting with Ms. Frazier and her students for three weeks of picture word lessons. Most of the lessons were conducted during their language arts time and lasted 30 minutes, a few about 45 minutes, and the unit will continue for at least another week. At reading time, Ms. Frazier will read them the first two pages of four informative books in which the authors have done masterful jobs with who, what, when, where, and how. During free reading time or for homework, she will ask students to select their favorite book from the Nonfiction Book Nook and be prepared to share with their partner and the group who, what, when, where, and how. Soon the group will write a paragraph about uniforms because the students find that to be one of the more interesting topics shaken out of the picture. After the group exercise, the students will write individual paragraphs about at least one of their categories of sentences. They will continue to add words to the chart and to their word wall, to work on spelling and phonics patterns; Ms. Frazier will continue to listen to them, to observe what they are producing, and to model and demonstrate and talk about how the English language works.

2

Describing the Picture
Word Inductive Model

> In this chapter, you'll find a definition of the picture word inductive model (PWIM), an outline of the general sequence of lessons when the full model is used, and a rationale for its use. While the PWIM has uses from primary through secondary school, this chapter focuses on using it with students at the emergent and beginning stages of literacy, especially those students in kindergarten through 2nd grade.

What?

The PWIM is an inquiry-oriented language arts strategy that uses pictures containing familiar objects and actions to elicit words from children's listening and speaking vocabularies. Teachers use the PWIM with classes, small groups, and individuals to lead them into inquiring about words, adding words to their sight-reading and writing vocabularies, discovering phonetic and structural principles, and using observation and analysis in their study of reading and writing.

Why?

The picture word inductive model can be used to teach phonics and spelling both inductively and explicitly. However, the model is designed to capitalize on children's ability to think inductively. The PWIM enables them to build generalizations that form the basis of structural and phonetic analysis. And it respects their ability to think. Thus, a major principle of the model is that students have the capability to make generalizations that can help them to master the conventions of language.

The instructional sequence of the model cycles and recycles through the following activities: The students study a picture selected by the teacher; identify what they see in the picture for the teacher to label; read and review the words generated; use the picture word chart to read their own sets of words; classify words according to properties they can identify; and develop titles, sentences, and paragraphs about their picture. Figure 2.1 shows the moves and the overall sequence of the model. The full sequence of a PWIM unit may take three days or two months: The length of units and number of lessons within a unit depend on the richness of the picture, the age and language development of the students, and the language objectives of the teacher.

For example, teachers using the model to develop sight-word vocabulary and to work on phonemic and graphemic awareness may stop at #7. Teachers who want to work with their students on reading and writing sentences and paragraphs use all the moves of the model. Teachers may recycle 4 through 9 completely or move backward or forward depending on student performance and the objectives for that lesson.

The picture word chart is the basic material for the PWIM lessons and units. The picture word chart comprises the picture and the words that are identified or "shaken out" of the picture by the students. The chart is used throughout the sequence of lessons and is a source of curriculum content. As the teacher writes words on the paper surrounding the picture, the chart becomes an illustrated dictionary. The dictionary supports language use by the class as a group and as individuals and needs to be posted where students can use it to support their reading, their writing, and their independence as learners. Using the chart to help them pronounce the words encourages children as young as 4 or 5

Figure 2.1—Overview of the Picture Word Inductive Model

Moves of the PWIM

1. Select a picture.
2. Ask students to identify what they see in the picture.
3. Label the picture parts identified. (Draw a line from the identified object or area, say the word, write the word; ask students to spell the word aloud and then to pronounce it.)
4. Read and review the picture word chart aloud.
5. Ask students to read the words (using the lines on the chart if necessary) and to classify the words into a variety of groups. Identify common concepts (e.g., beginning consonants, rhyming words) to emphasize with the whole class.
6. Read and review the picture word chart (say the word, spell it, say it again).
7. Add words, if desired, to the picture word chart and to the word banks.
8. Lead students into creating a title for the picture word chart. Ask students to think about the information on the chart and what they want to say about it.
9. Ask students to generate a sentence, sentences, or a paragraph about the picture word chart. Ask students to classify sentences; model putting the sentences into a good paragraph.
10. Read and review the sentences and paragraphs.

Strengths of the PWIM

The basic moves of the PWIM stress these components of phonics, grammar, mechanics, and usage:

• Students hear the words pronounced correctly many times and the picture word chart is an immediate reference as they add these words to their sight vocabulary. The teacher can choose to emphasize almost any sound and symbol relationship (introduced or taken to mastery).
• Students hear and see letters identified and written correctly many times.
• Students hear the words spelled correctly many times and participate in spelling them correctly.
• In writing the sentences, the teacher uses standard English (transforming student sentences if necessary) and uses correct punctuation and mechanics (e.g, commas, capital letters). As different mechanical and grammatical devices are used, the teacher describes why the device is used. After many lessons and experiences with the teacher modeling the devices, the students learn how to use them too.

years old to notice and comment on spelling and phonetic structure. Until the words are part of the student's sight vocabulary, they are anchored by their representations on the picture word chart.

For most beginning readers and writers, the PWIM is a satisfying and pleasurable activity: They enjoy finding objects and actions in the picture, seeing the words and sentences they generate expressed in print and become part of the curriculum, classifying words and sentences, and discovering useful language concepts and generalizations. The PWIM motivates students because most become successful learners. Learners succeed when using the model because the PWIM is based on inquiry into how children learn and how to enhance their learning, including their development of language, the process of learning to read and write, and the reading and writing connection.

Building on Language Development

By the time most children in the United States are 5 years old, they can listen to and speak 4,000 to 6,000 words with understanding and also use the basic syntactical structure of the language (Chall, 1967; Clark & Clark, 1977). They can listen with understanding to complex sentences and longer communications. They produce sentences that include prepositions and conjunctions and make causal connections like "If we go to the store now, we could watch 'Thomas the Tank Engine' when we get back." They gobble up words, play with them, and have conversations with stuffed animals and dolls—composing ideas and manipulating words much as they will when they begin to write. Children's natural acquisition of language is a dimension of culture and brings with it a great sense of personal power and satisfaction as young learners receive communications and learn to put their ideas into words.

The picture word inductive model builds on the listening and speaking vocabularies of the students, helping them to add reading and writing to their communications repertoire. The concept of using pictures as a stimulus for language experience activities in the class-room was developed specifically for teaching young students to read and write (e.g., see Adams, Johnson, & Connors, 1980). In the struc-ture of the picture word inductive model, young children are presented with pictures of familiar scenes or photographs of everyday items. They shake out words from the picture by identifying objects, actions, and qualities they recognize in the picture. The words or phrases the stu-dents use to identify the objects, actions, or qualities are connected to words already in their naturally developed listening and speaking vocabularies. The next step occurs as the teacher draws a line from the object to the surrounding paper and writes the word or phrase.

Both the process (moves) and the structure of the model respect children's language development and enable them to begin reading by using their language in conjunction with the pictures. The PWIM is designed to enable students to be immediately successful as language learners in the formal school setting and to immerse them in how lan-guage works.

The connections between the children's language and the items and actions in the picture support the transition from oral (listened to and spoken) language to written (read and written) language. Students witness the transformation from oral to written expression. They watch the words being spelled and spell them with the teacher. They connect something in the picture with a word and then watch that word appear as letters. They can now read that word. Shortly, they learn that we always spell that word the same way. They identify a dog in the picture, see *dog* written, hear it spelled, spell it themselves, and on the way home from school they see a Lost Dog poster on the street corner and read the word again.

How does the PWIM and children's development of language relate to the current emphasis on brain-compatible teaching and learn-ing? The instructional environment created by the teacher through the PWIM is probably closest to the position articulated by Ramey and

Ramey (1998). These professors and researchers offer six "developmental priming mechanisms" repeatedly associated with "positive cognitive, social, and emotional outcomes of children" (Ramey & Ramey, 1998, p. 115) (and probably also with the continuing development of adults):

- Encouragement of exploration,
- Mentoring in basic cognitive and social skills,
- Celebrating new skills,
- Guided rehearsal and extension of new skills,
- Protection from inappropriate punishment or ridicule for developmental advances, and
- Stimulation in language and symbolic communication.

(Ramey & Ramey, 1998, p. 115)

According to Ramey and Ramey, the priming mechanisms need to be present in children's lives on a frequent and predictable basis. The framework of the PWIM addresses five of the six priming mechanisms for continued development. Meanwhile, we continue to learn about education and the brain and what is needed to support language development and literacy (Education Commission of the States & The Charles A. Dana Foundation, 1996; Bruer, 1997).

A major principle of the picture word inductive model is to build on children's growing storehouse of spoken and understood words and syntactic forms and facilitate the transition to writing and reading. Most children want to make sense of the language around them and they eagerly engage in unlocking its mysteries. A corollary principle of the PWIM is that the approach respects the children's language development: Their words are used and their ability to make connections is central to the learning process and the model.

Stimulating Reading and Writing Skills

Much remains to be learned about the almost magical process whereby children make connections between their naturally developing language and the world of reading and writing. Our understanding is that several types of learning need to be accomplished to develop reading and writing skills.

Children must build a substantial sight vocabulary—a storehouse of words instantly recognizable by their spellings. We want students reading books as soon as possible for many reasons: for literacy acquisition; for skills practice; for their self-esteem as learners; and for developing a sense of literate behavior that comes through being able to independently access the ideas of others through the alphabetic code of their native language (as in "I can read this book! Hear me!"). About 100 words bring simple books like *Go, Dog, Go* (Eastman, 1961) within reach. Also, once students have about 50 sight words, their study of phonics is greatly facilitated, as are many other aspects of learning, including the development of more vocabulary (Graves, Watts, & Graves, 1994). About 450 words bring children to the stage in which many picture storybooks are available to them.

The picture word inductive model approaches the development of sight vocabulary directly. The students read and spell the words that are shaken out of the picture. Then, these words are placed on large word cards that they can look at and the teacher can use for group instruction. Students also get their own set of word cards. They sort these words and consult the picture dictionary to check their understanding and refresh the meaning of the words. The students keep word cards in envelopes, word banks, or word boxes, consulting them as they wish and eventually using the cards and words to compose sentences.

Children must build concepts about the conventions used in language to connect sounds and structures to print forms. The repeated instructional pattern as words are added to the chart and reviewed—see the item, say the word, listen as the teacher spells the word, read the word as a group, spell it together, read the word again—teaches and reinforces letter recognition, as well as the pronunciation of the words, while repeated attention to the words and spelling helps to build students' reading and writing vocabularies.

With respect to sound and print forms (phonetic, often called sound-and-symbol or letter-and-sound relationships), children need to learn that nearly all words that begin with a particular sound begin with particular letters that represent that sound. Periodically, a teacher using the PWIM will ask students to pull out all the words they have in their word bank that contain a *b* and they will concentrate on that letter. Another time, *at* will get attention. After the students have learned to read most of the words on the picture chart, the teacher may ask them to pull out all the words in which they can hear /s/. Thus, phonetic and structural analysis skills are learned through developing concepts and applying them to the reading and writing process.

The PWIM can help students learn about the structure of words as they build an understanding of inflection, the change of form that words undergo to indicate number, gender, person, tense, case, mood, or voice. For instance, in Chapter 1, Ms. Tayloe directed her kindergarten students to notice the similarities and differences between singular and plural words, specifically how *apple* and *apples* are alike and different. Although it may seem impossible for students to believe, structural conventions eventually result in more rapid and accurate communication of their ideas.

The picture word inductive model induces students to classify their words, building the concepts that enable them to unlock unfamiliar words. The English language has about 44 sounds represented in more than 200 forms—some say as many as 250 forms (Morris, 1997—because some have multiple representations: /sh/ut, na/tion/. As students work with their words, they develop categories: these words all begin like *boy*; these words all have two *d*'s in the middle like *ladder*. Students develop word families that they can use to read and spell words they have not memorized; for instance, the word family of *bat*, *cat*, and *hat* can be used to help read and spell *mat*. And, they learn that the generalizations they make will enable them to unlock about 70 percent of the new words they encounter.

Students will be amused at some of the ways we spell words such as *ate* and *eight*, and will sigh occasionally at our insistence that they learn the peculiarities our language has developed. They will be perplexed by *see* and *sea* and want to know why we made them sound alike. At times, all we can say is what our teachers said to us, "You'll just have to memorize them."

Strengthening the Reading and Writing Connection

Reading and writing are naturally connected, can be learned simultaneously, and can be used together to rapidly and effectively advance growth in language use (Stotsky, 1983; Tierney & Pearson, 1985; Hillocks, 1987; Shanahan, 1988, 1990; and Heller, 1991). How is the reading and writing connection used in the PWIM? As the students search a picture for items and objects they can identify with words or phrases, the teacher writes their words on the picture word chart, which launches the students into the early stages of formal writing. Later, the students make up short sentences about the picture and begin to write longer sentences and then paragraphs with the help of the teacher. Through repetition, the words in the sentences are added to their storehouse of knowledge.

Gradually, as the students read more trade books, they learn to analyze how others write and they begin to use the conventional writing devices to enhance their ability to express themselves. Essentially, they come to use the library of the world as models for sharing and communicating ideas through writing. As they read picture storybooks and short informative books, they discuss them by making up sentences about the book. Many students begin to feel that their reading is not complete until they have said something about the book in their own words, completing the communication loop between the author and the reader.

Beginning in kindergarten, students and teachers work together building words and sentences and paragraphs and books. As they build paragraphs, they select and discuss titles. The teacher leads metacognitive discussions on choosing titles and talks to the students about which title is most comprehensive, which title might be most interesting to one audience or another, which sentences go with one title, which with another. When writing a paragraph or creating a title, the teacher helps students to focus on the essence of communication: What do we want to say to our readers? to ourselves? Focusing on communication is what Mrs. Frazier and her 2nd grade students were doing in their lessons. Her students use the reading and writing connection as she has them think about what they want to share, what they most want the reader to know, and how to help the reader get this information. The reading and writing connection culminates as the class evaluates their effectiveness in sharing what they wished to share. Mrs. Frazier continues to work on this link until it becomes explicit and accessible for the students to use as independent learners.

▼   ▼   ▼

The picture word inductive model is designed to teach reading, writing, and the language system. It is designed to help students develop as independent learners and as independent readers and to foster confidence based on knowledge that they secure for themselves as learners. Within each class, students' language development will vary as will their confidence in participating. Given time, many experiences with the model, and a nurturing and joyous learning environment, most students—not just the quickest or most language agile students—make good progress as readers and writers.

3

Using the Model
in a Language Arts Unit

In this scenario, we visit with Velma Lewis and her 1st grade students for three weeks. Mrs. Lewis's class moves through the model in the same way that Ms. Tayloe's class did in Chapter 1. The same kinds of questions and ideas are generated as the class shakes words out of the picture of a sports equipment room. Note the similarities in how the PWIM is used with students from kindergarten through 2nd grade. As you read this, see if you can feel the sequence of the model and the continuous diagnosis into language learning that is similar across grade levels.

Mrs. Lewis's 6-year-olds at Washington Primary School are working on building their reading and writing vocabularies. They are also working on their phonics and spelling skills by analyzing the structures of words that are in their listening, speaking, and reading vocabularies.

After working for several days with a picture of a sports equipment storage room, they have created an illustrated dictionary (picture word chart) by shaking out words from the picture. Mrs. Lewis has supplied the words to each student on word cards. She gives each child a set with

22 of the more than 50 words shaken out of the picture; she will add the other cards later.

This lesson from the fourth day of the PWIM unit opens with students reading the words on the picture word chart (Figure 3.1). Then Mrs. Lewis takes out six word cards that she has selected for special attention. These words are written in large print on sentence strips (larger versions of the word cards). In yesterday's lesson, these six words and phrases were among the most frequently "read" words at the picture word chart, probably because they were on top of the stack in the envelope: *baseball, baseball bat, football, yellow football, basketball,* and *ball.* Today, the group practices locating each word visually on the chart, and then Mrs. Lewis calls on a student to match the word on the sentence strip to the word on the picture word chart. The other students raise their hands if they agree with the match, then the group reads and spells the word aloud. Mrs. Lewis goes through the process for each word and then places the six word cards in the pocket chart. Her pocket chart is a posterboard with clear plastic pockets that she can slide words and sentence strips into. The words are written large enough to be viewed by the whole class.

Mrs. Lewis says to the students, "Look carefully at the words in our pocket chart. Think silently. What do you notice about them?"

Figure 3.1—1st Graders Identify Words for Curriculum

football	two posters
basketball	books
Mickey Mouse	window
poster	storage room
basket	baseball bat
yellow football	chair
three basketballs	two windows
balloon	baseball
basket	baseballs
little football	chair
big green ball	ball
wagon	broom
baskets	box
water bottle	two chairs
red wagon	plastic bats
basketball	brooms
book	lights
cheering teddy bear	hooks
small wagon	bucket
room	poster

Tommy says that he can read all of them, and Jordan notices that all of the words have letters. Chaminade observes that the list contains two "baseballs." Miranda says *baseball, football, basketball,* and *ball* all have *ball* in them. And Louis blurts out that the words all have two *l*'s at the end. Mrs. Lewis asks Miranda to arrange those words in a column on the pocket chart and then says. "Watch carefully as Miranda points out *ball* in *baseball, football,* and *basketball*." Miranda points out *ball* in each word and returns to her seat.

Then Mrs. Lewis says, "Louis, you were being a good word detective. These four words, let's read them together . . . all have two *l*'s. We cannot write *ball*, b-a-l-l, or any word with *ball* in it without using two *l*'s. Let me hear everyone spell *ball*."

"B-a-l-l," the class shouts.

"Study the letters in *ball* carefully, only those four letters, in that order, will spell the word *ball* in English," says Mrs. Lewis. She specifically mentions spelling in English because the class has discussed different languages and they have learned four or five Arabic words from a classmate whose parents speak Arabic and English.

Mrs. Lewis pulls out two word cards, *bat* and *yellow,* that students do not have as separate word cards. She says, "Everyone look carefully at these words. When you think you know what they are, raise your hand."

Jordan responds to the teacher's prompt by saying, "*Bat,* the short one is *bat*."

"Good reading, Jordan. Can you come up and point to the word *bat* on a word card in our pocket chart?" Jordan comes up and points to the word *bat* on the word card that says *baseball bat.*

"Now, this one," Mrs. Lewis says holding up the card with *yellow* written on it. She gives students a minute and calls on Jessica.

"*Yellow football,*" says Jessica.

Mrs. Lewis takes the word card for *football* out of the pocket chart and says, "Now, everyone watch and listen carefully. Think silently, do not blurt out. What is this word, Jessica?"

"*Yellow football.*"

Mrs. Lewis hands Jessica the word card and says, "Jessica, would you place this word right under its match on the chart?" Jessica gets up, walks to the charts, pauses a moment, and places the word card under *football* in the phrase *yellow football.*

"Good reading," says Mrs. Lewis. "What is that word?"

"*Football,*" says Jessica.

"And what color is this football?"

"*Yellow.*"

"Can you put your hand under *yellow?*" Jessica points out the word and returns to her seat.

Mrs. Lewis places the card with *yellow football* on the left side of the pocket chart and says to the students, "We have two separate words on this card, *yellow,*" placing one hand under *yellow,* "and *football.*" Then she places the word cards *yellow* and *football* one under the other in the pocket chart.

"Does anyone see another card in our list with two separate words?" The students identify *baseball bat,* and they spend a few minutes on those words.

Mrs. Lewis's experience has taught her to stop the lessons at appropriate conceptual loop or lesson loop times, to stop when the students have been engaged for a long time (more than 30 minutes), and to stop when they get too squirmy because it's time to go to the media center, lunch, or music. At this point, she finishes this segment of the lesson by saying, "I am going to leave our six word cards in the pocket today. Study them, practice reading them, and see if you notice anything else about them."

They have been focusing on the six sight words and phrases that are to be mastered by everyone. Today's activities have provided additional practice in reading and spelling these six words and focused students' attention on the similarities and differences among these words.

Recognizing similarities and differences helps students learn to read these words and helps them to classify words according to their structural and phonetic properties.

The following morning, Mrs. Lewis reviews the picture word chart with the children, reading and spelling the words together. They review the six word cards and Mrs. Lewis decides to work with the students on discriminating singular and plural words because she noticed that some students were reading *book* as *books* and *hook* as *hooks*. She does this to move students toward recognizing the concept of singular and plural and how *-s* works in forming many plural nouns.

Mrs. Lewis uses the flip chart and begins the lesson by leading students in brief silent and oral reading practice on these words, similar to what they did with the six words in yesterday's lesson. Several students eagerly share that *book*, *books*, *hook*, and *hooks* all have two letters just alike, side by side. Part of the visual study and practice in this segment of the lesson emphasizes how to discriminate *book* from *books* and *hook* from *hooks*, with work on the sounds represented by *b* and *h*, some work on the /o͝o/ sound as in *book* and *hook*. Discussion of rhyming words (students generate several additional words that rhyme—*look*, *looks*, *cook*, and *cooks*), and some discussion of how *-s* by itself at the end of a word often indicates more than one object. Their homework is to see if they can find other words that rhyme with *book* or *books*.

The next day, the lesson begins with a silent reading of all the words on the chart and the teacher calling on students to read them aloud. Then she reviews the two sets of special study words followed by a check on homework discoveries. They add *took* and *shook* to the flip chart. Now the list includes *book*, *books*, *hook*, *hooks*, *look*, *looks*, *cook*, *cooks*, *took*, *shook*. They spend a few minutes developing meaning for *took* and *shook*. Although most students know what *took* means, Mrs. Lewis demonstrates its meaning by taking things from several students and describing her action in a sentence, *I took Brian's book*. She writes the sentence on the board, reads it, and has the students read it. Mrs. Lewis does one demonstration for *shook*, "I shook my head." Mitch comes up with "The puppy shook mud all over me."

Angela suggests adding *tooks* and *shooks* to the flip chart. The teacher responds that Angela's idea makes sense and fits a pattern, and she reads and points to *book, books, hook, hooks, look, looks, cook, cooks*. Mrs. Lewis explains, however, that "*tooks* and *shooks* did not become words in our language. We use *takes* and *shakes* instead." Mrs. Lewis does not take this line of reasoning any further; she does not believe her beginning 1st graders are ready for conjugating irregular verbs with any level of conceptual understanding. She may explain this concept later, or with another group of students, or with a smaller group.

Mrs. Lewis begins to prepare her students for classifying their words. She briefly reviews what they have been working on in math: sorting their red cubes from their green triangles and making patterns. She holds a set of pattern blocks of various colors and shapes in a small tray and asks the students to look at them. Then she says, "Watch carefully, see if you can be a very good detective. I am going to select three of these that go together. Your job as a detective is to think of as many reasons as you can why they go together." Mrs. Lewis selects three green triangular shapes and asks the students to think about how these three are alike. She gives students a minute to study. The students respond that

- They're all green;
- They all have three sides;
- They are pattern blocks;
- On Saturday we went to the store to look for some;
- Three points; and
- Green triangles!

Mrs. Lewis remarks that they are all good detectives and asks if a green square fits the group. Ricky explains that it is not a triangle. Jake takes Ricky's thoughts and expresses the idea that a square has four sides; Annalyn says that it can't belong because it's a square, triangles have three sides. Another student comments that it is shaped like the roof of a house.

"You're right. This pattern block does not belong in my set because it has more than three sides. It is not a triangle. Now look carefully." Mrs. Lewis holds up a red triangle and asks the student if it would fit her group.

Angela explains that it doesn't fit because it's a red triangle. Mrs. Lewis responds, "What good detectives you are. You noticed that the pattern blocks in my set were all green, had three sides, had three points, and are called triangles. You have been using a very important thinking skill called classifying. Let's do one more practice classifying together before you do it by yourselves. Watch carefully."

Mrs. Lewis picks up the large name cards the class uses as she takes attendance. She calls Jake to the front and hands his name card to him, and repeats the pattern with Jordan, Jeanette, and Jessica. Mrs. Lewis asks the class to study each name card carefully and figure out how they are alike. She gives them a minute to think silently and then she asks for responses:
- They're all kids;
- They're all in 1st grade;
- Two boys and two girls;
- They all have *j*'s; and
- They're all alike at the start.

Mrs. Lewis asks Bruce to point to where the names are "all alike," and he does. The class is asked to agree with Bruce or not, and then Mrs. Lewis writes a *J* on the chart nearby. She explains that *Jake, Jordan, Jeanette,* and *Jessica* all begin with the same letter. Jessica can't stand it any longer and blurts out, "It's a *j*!"

Mrs. Lewis calls on Louis who has been waving his hand energetically but patiently for several minutes. "Thanks for waiting quietly, Louis."

Louis gets up and walks up to the cards. He points to the *j* and *a* in each word and says, "They all have J's and A's."

Mrs. Lewis says, "Everyone watch carefully. Louis, would you point to those letters again?" Louis does so and returns to his seat. Mrs. Lewis collects the name cards from the students and places them in the pocket chart, "Thank you, Jeanette, Jordan, Jessica, and Jake."

Mrs. Lewis, holding up Chaminade's name card, asks, "Would this name fit in our group?" She calls on several students who give varying but correct responses about why it could not belong. Then she holds up Jackie's name card, students easily identify it as a member of the group. Mrs. Lewis places it in the pocket chart and helps her students think about writing and spelling by saying, as she points to the *j* in each name, "Yes, if we want to write Jeanette's, Jordan's, Jessica's, Jake's, or Jackie's name, we have to begin it with an uppercase or capital *J*."

She brings the group practice to a close and reinforces and extends the students comments and thinking by saying, "You were good detectives. I did put these names together because they all begin with *j*. I did not think about *a* being in every name, but Louis spotted it. Tomorrow, you'll begin to classify the words in your envelopes. So be sure to study all the words on the chart—how they are spelled and how they sound. That will help you become a super classification detective."

Mrs. Lewis brings her students into formal classification of words by connecting the classification work they have done in forming groups and sets and working on shapes in mathematics. She begins with objects that are tangible and concrete (the pattern blocks); then moves them to relatively familiar words (their names), and then on to looking at the letters in their new words. She had planned for students to begin classifying their words today, but the lesson had gone on long enough.

When the students arrive at the picture word area the next day, the flip chart is turned to their *book, books, took* list. Mrs. Lewis directs them to see how many of the words they can read, working silently, then she reads the words aloud for the students to check their reading.

Then she says, "Now watch carefully. I am going to make another set of words, a set of words that go together." She writes *book, hook, look, cook, shook* on the other side of the flip chart, reads them aloud slowly, and says, "I put these words together because they all have the /o͞o/ in them and they all rhyme. Let's read them together and listen to the /o͞o/ and to the rhyme." The class reads the list of words aloud and then Mrs. Lewis leads them into classifying the words from the *book, books, took* list. The class adds *took* to the list.

She moves the students into their first independent classification of the words from the chart. Each student has a set of cards and is fully engaged in studying the words. Mrs. Lewis asks the students to find some words that go together because they are alike in some way. Students find their personal space and spread out their cards. There is a regular stream of traffic as students go to the picture chart to check their reading. Mrs. Lewis walks around the room observing and asking students about their word groups.

The students are given 15 minutes to work individually on reading and classifying their words. Some students read their words to her when they describe their group; others do not. Some students identify the likenesses by pointing and saying that their words have the same two letters in them. Mrs. Lewis extends their learning by pointing to these letters and saying, "You're right: *ball, baseball, small wagon, baseball bat* all have two *l*'s in them. Can you find any more words with two *l*'s in them?"

A few students are still practicing their reading, so Mrs. Lewis praises them for their good reading and asks them to see if they can find at least two words that go together for some reason. She ends the lesson by having the class read the words on the chart aloud.

Mrs. Lewis begins the next lesson on reading, studying, and classifying words by asking the students to pay close attention to which letters go together to make up a particular word. Mrs. Lewis reminds the students that the more carefully they study a word—and how the letters fit together—the more likely they are to recognize it the next time. She gives them examples, beginning with placing *bat* and *ball* in a column on the pocket chart. Mrs. Lewis asks them to study the two words and to raise their hands when they have something to share about them. She waits until most hands are up and calls on Tommy, who identifies the words as *bat* and *ball*. Mrs. Lewis asks him how he knows that, and Tommy responds by matching the word cards from the pocket chart to the picture word chart.

Marvina observes, "*Bat* starts with *b* and so does *ball*."

Jessica interrupts with, "And they're short, they're little words."

Mrs. Lewis adds *basket* to the pocket chart under *bat* and *ball*. She says, "Study these three words. Read them silently. When you have something to share about them, raise your hand." She waits until most hands are up and calls on Miranda.

"They all have *b* first," says Miranda. Mrs. Lewis asks Miranda to come up and show everyone the *b* at the beginning of each word. Then she calls on Brian.

"They all have *b*'s and *a*'s at the first," says Brian.

Mrs. Lewis leads students in activities that help them notice and attend to the characteristics of words and the order of letters. For example, she shows them that specific letters form one word and that if only one letter is added, it is a different word; the concept that a letter often makes the same sound (as in *b* in *bat*, *ball*, and *basket*); and that letters can affect each other's sounds, as in *bat* and *ball*.

Mrs. Lewis has the students continue classifying their words just as they did in yesterday's lesson, but she requests that they "find some words that go together because they are alike in some way and be ready to tell us why. See if you can come up with some new groups, different from yesterday's groups."

Students find their personal space and spread out their cards. As yesterday, there is a regular stream of traffic as students go over to the picture word chart to check their reading. Mrs. Lewis walks around observing and asking students about their groups. Mrs. Lewis has students classify their words several times because she believes students can discover much about how our language works from classifying the same list of words, a valuable lesson in learning that there is more than one correct answer. The use of the same list of words encourages the students to learn to continue inquiring to see what else they might discover.

After 20 minutes, Mrs. Lewis asks the students to share some of their categories with the class. She calls for the students to pay attention as a group, but asks them to remain in their personal spaces to facilitate access to their word cards, "Here we go! More tough stuff! As we share our groups, I want you to practice listening to each other very carefully. That means you have to do a lot of silent thinking. See what you can learn about our words from listening to each other. Select your favorite group and get ready to share it with everyone: First, put the words in that group together; and second, be ready to share why you put them together."

Mrs. Lewis sets up the physical environment to facilitate student use of the learning community and the social setting. She does this by helping students who can't see the pocket chart to turn their bodies or chairs or to find new spaces. She wants them to learn how to learn from each other. She works to prepare and organize the students to help them participate in oral discourse as members of a large group.

While the students are organizing their groups, Mrs. Lewis places her set of word cards in one side of the pocket chart. Then she looks around to make sure everyone has at least one group ready, and calls on Marius to read the words in his set.

Marius reads aloud his set: *two posters, three basketballs, two windows.* Marius explains that they all have numbers. While Marius reads his set, Mrs. Lewis places her large version of the word cards that

Marius is reading on the pocket chart for the class to view. After that, the teacher asks the class to review the set and come up with ways in which the words are alike. In this way, all students practice studying groups other than their own and deduce why those items have been placed together. She calls on Jackie who says that the word cards all begin with *t*.

Mrs. Lewis says, "That's right, Jackie, all three words, *two*, *three*, and *two* have *t* as the first letter. Does everyone see the *t*'s?"

Louis blurts out, "I see more *t*'s!"

"Juwan, can you come up and point out the *t*'s at the beginning of *two*, *three*, and *two* for us," prompts Mrs. Lewis. Juwan complies and Mrs. Lewis asks him, "Do you see any other *t*'s?" Juwan studies the words for a moment, points to the *t* in *poster* and in *basketball*, and returns to his seat. Mrs. Lewis calls on Jeanette.

Jeanette answers, "All have tall letters."

Mrs. Lewis, "Jeanette, would you come up and show us?" Jeanette walks up and points to the *t* in *two*, *posters*; the *t* and the *h* in *three*, and the *b*, *k*, *t*, and two *l*'s in *basketball*; the *t* in *two* and the *d* in *windows*. Mrs. Lewis says, "Thank you, Jeanette." Pointing to the words and letters, she says, "*Two* begins with tall letter *t*, *poster* has tall letter *t* in the middle, *three* begins with tall letters *t* and *h*. How many tall letters in the word *basketball*?" The students take a moment then respond and they move on to *two windows*. Mrs. Lewis closes this conceptual loop by saying, "When we are writing these letters, we make them taller than our *w*'s, *o*'s, *s*'s and *e*'s."

Mrs. Lewis is teaching the students to attend to the formation of letters. As part of their work with the picture word inductive model, students will see and discuss the formation of the twenty-six letters of the alphabet many times and they will discuss the sounds represented by each letter.

Jordan is waving his arm and bouncing up and down and blurts out, "They all have two words."

"Who agrees with Jordan?" asks Mrs. Lewis. Most of the students raise their hands and she calls on Selena to point out the two words on each card. Then she calls on Jake.

"There are three words in *three basketballs*," says Jake.

Mrs. Lewis invites Jake to come up and point out the three words, then she says, "*Basketball* is a special kind of word. Sometimes in our language we put two words together to make one word that means something very different. Often the first word says something about how the second word is used." She turns and points to the basketball on the picture chart, "Why do you think this is called a *basketball?* What does *basket* tell us about *ball?*" She gives them a minute to think about it. Several hands go up, and Mrs. Lewis calls on Chris.

Chris says, "Because you try to put it in the basket." They discuss the game of basketball for a few minutes and Mrs. Lewis brings this lesson to a close by complimenting the class on their work and asking the students to study the chart and find more examples of two words written together to mean one thing.

Mrs. Lewis made an intentional decision to stay with the one group of words shared by Marius despite her goal of sharing words classified by four or five students. Each year she has to remind herself to slow down and to allow the students to think and analyze the words they generate. She understands that the students need to take time to study what they already know and where they are as readers, writers, and spellers—individually and as a group.

Mrs. Lewis opens the next lesson by saying, "Today, I want everyone to practice reading all the words on our chart silently. I'll put my hand under each word, give you a few seconds to read it, then trace the line to the picture so you can check your reading." After that, the teacher provides another example of classification, leads students into analyzing the characteristics of the group, and takes the opportunity to work on plurals and on how -s works to form plural nouns.

"Who remembers what that long word *clas/si/fy/ing* means?" asks Mrs. Lewis as she slowly pronounces the word and writes it on the board.

Miranda blurts out, "It has two *s*'s just like *grass*."

Mrs. Lewis responds by saying, "It does have two *s*'s just like *grass*. When we spell *classify* or *grass* we use two *s*'s side-by-side. But think some more, you're thinking about how it's spelled, can anyone tell us what it means?" A few hands go up, but Mrs. Lewis decides to demonstrate instead of risking a series of guesses. She looks at the word cards and selects *baskets*, *bottles*, and *posters*, placing them one under the other in a small pocket chart. "I just classified these words—out of all our words, I chose these three words and put them together for a reason. Study them a minute, see if you can discover why I put them together." She waits, then calls on Jake.

"You put them together 'cause they all have *s*'s at the end," said Jake proudly.

"You're right, Jake. That is one of the reasons I put them together," responds Mrs. Lewis, before calling on Jan.

"They're all some," explains Jan.

"Can you say more about that, Jan? What do you mean when you say 'some'?"

"Some baskets, some bottles, and two posters, not just one."

"Good thinking, Jan. That is also one of the reasons I put these words together." Mrs. Lewis points to and reads *baskets*, *bottles*, and *posters*, "I put these words together—I classified them into one group—because they all have an *s* at the end that tells me they mean more than one basket, more than one bottle, and more than one poster. Just like Jake and Miranda discovered. Let's study these *s*'s a bit more." Mrs. Lewis finds her word cards for *basket*, *bottle*, and *poster*, and places *basket* and *baskets* one under the other in the pocket chart. Let's look at *basket* and *baskets*. How are they the same and how are they different?" Several children volunteer, and she calls on Theo.

"They're spelled the same except for the ess sound on the end," says

Theo.

"Which one has the ess sound, Theo, *basket* or *baskets?*" asks Mrs. Lewis.

"*Baskets!*" shouts Theo.

Louis can't stand it any longer: "S, *baskets* has an *s*. And *basket* is just one basket and *baskets* are lots of baskets."

Mrs. Lewis confirms Louis's identification of *-s* and that at the end of these words it means more than one item. She decides to extend her comments to words not on the chart. "For many words—many nouns like *ball* and *basket*, for example—when we want to make them mean more than one, we can just add an *-s*."

Mrs. Lewis writes *girl* and *girls* one under the other and some of the students shout out "*girls*"; she writes *boy* and *boys* one under the other and some shout "*boys*."

"Think hard. Who can come up and point to the one that means more than one girl and tell us why?" They work quickly through the exercise and move to their personal spaces and begin reading and classifying their words. This time Mrs. Lewis has students work as partners. She walks around with her pad, taking notes about the classifications the students are forming, making sure that students are reading their words or visiting the picture word chart if they need to, making comments, and leading students into adding to their classifications and articulating their reasons for putting words together. After 15 minutes, Mrs. Lewis has a list of useful categories. She calls a halt to the classification activity and asks everyone to turn so they can see the pocket chart and the flip chart.

Mrs. Lewis says, "Now watch closely. I am going to put together some groups of words like those I saw you put together. Sometime today—when we have quiet time or if you finish your center time early—see if you can read these words and figure out why partners put each set of words together." Mrs. Lewis forms groups (see Figure 3.2) and leaves them in the large pocket chart.

"How many of you studied our word lists yesterday or this morning?" asks Mrs. Lewis. Everyone raises a hand. "Look at our first list, Set 1 [Figure 3.2]. Who knows why these words are together?"

They begin to analyze Set 1 and to discuss its attributes. Students find additional words on the chart that can be added to the sets. Mrs. Lewis has them think, look around the room, and come up with other words to add. They add *badge*, *band*, and *bug* to the set of words with initial consonant *b*; *softball*, *bookcase*, *bookshelf*, *book-shelves*, and *desktop* to the set of compound words. Mrs. Lewis places a question mark beside *desktop* because she's not certain if it is written as two words or as one. They check the dictionary and find it is written as one word. Mrs. Lewis

Figure 3.2—Teacher's Example of Categorizing Words

Set 1	Set 2	Set 3
baseball	football	little
box	baseball	bottle
baskets	basketball	
ball		
basketball		
basketballs		
bottle		
books		

does not explain the difference between its uses as a noun or adjective.

Mrs. Lewis decides the lesson has lasted long enough, "You've been such good listeners and had so many good ideas about how letters and words work. We'll come back to our chart after center time. Let's stand up, get some wiggle room, and have some music and exercise." She turns on one of their favorite songs.

Later in the day they begin again with the picture word inductive model by quickly reading the three sets of words. Then they begin working on Set 3, *little* and *bottle*. Mrs. Lewis writes *little* and *bottle* on the flip chart and asks, "Why did we put these two words from our chart into a set?" The students respond

- Two letters just alike in the middle;
- They have six letters;
- They have two parts;

- They have three tall letters in the middle;
- The *e* sounds invisible; and
- They all end in *-le.*

Mrs. Lewis selects some of their responses for extension. She says, "Hold on, that's enough. Everything you said about these two words is 100 percent correct. These two letters just alike in the middle [pointing to the *t*'s and *d*'s] are two of our consonants. Who can tell us something about consonants?"

Ricky, pointing to the D'Nealian alphabet cards posted along the bottom of the bulletin board near the writing center, explains, "They're the ones with no red lines. Vowels have red lines under them."

"Yeah, like the letter strips at our table," inserts Louis.

"When a word has two consonants just alike in the middle—it also has at least two parts," explains Mrs. Lewis. She says the two words, emphasizing each syllable slightly. She asks the students to read them aloud together and to clap their hands for each part.

They add *rattle* and *tattle* to the set of two syllable words formed with double consonants, in this set two *t*'s, followed by *-le.*

Mrs. Lewis writes *door* on the whiteboard; several students pronounce it. The teacher asks if the word belongs in the group and calls on Selena.

"Uh-huh," says Selena.

"Why?" asks Mrs. Lewis.

"Because it has two letters the same in the middle."

"But they're short letters," interjects Chaminade.

"They're vowels, not consonants, and there's no *-le* at the end," Mitch says smugly.

Mrs. Lewis, pointing to the letters in *door*, says, "As Selena noticed, there are two letters the same in the middle, two *o*'s. And as Chaminade pointed out, they are both short letters. But, this word does not belong in this group because, as Mitch said, these *o*'s are vowels, not consonants, and there is no *-le* at the end of the word. Raise your hand if you can read this word." About two-thirds of the students raise their hands. Mrs. Lewis calls on Theo, who has his hand up. Theo says, "*Door*, because d-o-o-r spells *door*."

Mrs. Lewis calls on Omar, who says that he can read it because it's on the door. Omar demonstrates by walking to the front door, the back door, and the two cabinet doors—he points out that each has *door* posted on it.

The next day, Marius begins the lesson by leading the class in reading all the words on the chart. Then Mrs. Lewis asks about their homework, finding words that would belong in Set 3 with *little* and *bottle*.

Marvina suggests they add *cattle*. Mrs. Lewis writes and spells *cattle* on the flip chart, then says, "Everyone, look carefully at the word *cattle*. Would *cattle* belong to the group with *little*, *bottle*, *rattle*, and *tattle?*" Most students assure her it would, and she calls on Marvina to talk about why *cattle* would be a member of this group.

Tommy volunteers *battle*. Mrs. Lewis asks the class what *battle* begins with, then calls on Jake to spell it as she writes it on the board. They briefly discuss why it belongs in Set 3. Andrea remarks that it could also belong in the set with the *b* words, so Mrs. Lewis adds it to Set 1.

Annalyn suggests they add *riddle*, so the teacher writes and spells *little* and *bottle* one under the other on the white board, moves over some and writes and spells *riddle* and *middle*, one under the other, and asks students to study the four words. "What do you notice? What is alike about these four words?" The students quickly identify the similarities, and Mrs. Lewis emphasizes the two identical consonants in the middle followed by -*le*, forming words with two syllables. Then she asks students to focus on the differences:

• *Little* and *bottle* have two *t*'s, *riddle* and *middle* have two *d*'s in the middle.

• *Bottle* has an *o*.

• *Riddle* and *middle* are spelled just alike, but the first letter is different. They sound alike.

Mrs. Lewis asks them to look at Set 3 and reads the words to them, then says, "If we describe Set 3 as having words with two consonants just alike in the middle, followed by *-le*, and having two parts, two syllables, then *riddle* and *middle* would belong in the set. But . . . you said earlier, that all the items in this set had two *t*'s side-by-side in the middle." They decide to make a separate set. Mrs. Lewis works with them briefly on rhyming words and on the different sounds represented by *t* and *d* and on the pronunciation differences between *little* and *riddle*, and the lesson ends.

The next day, Mrs. Lewis announces, "Today we are going to focus on sentences." She writes *sentence* and *sentences* on the board to formally introduce the concept of sentence.

"We're going to write sentences about our picture. Instead of telling us what an object is in our picture, like *football* or *yellow football*, you can tell us something more about the picture, like we have here." Mrs. Lewis picks up a sentence card from the class's previous picture word inductive model. "Who can read this sentence? Jordan?"

"Watch while I write another sentence about our picture." Mrs. Lewis turns, looks at the picture for a moment, and writes *There are two posters in the room, a Mickey Mouse poster and a teddy bear poster.* She pauses and asks, "Who sees some words in my sentence that they can read?" Hands go up and she calls on several students who identify *teddy bear, Mickey Mouse, two,* and *posters.* Then she reads the sentence and has the students read it with her. "Now, who has another sentence for us? Everyone listen carefully."

Mrs. Lewis began by using the short sentence that students were familiar with; created a new sentence as a model for the meaning of sentence; provided an opportunity for students to practice reading their sight words within the sentences and to celebrate their growing skill in reading; and continued to help students notice that letters make up words and words make up sentences.

As a student shares a sentence, Mrs. Lewis listens, repeats it orally for clarification and volume, writes it pronouncing each word as she goes, jots down the initials of the author, and finally has all the students read it aloud with her. Here are some of the sentences:

- There are some old jackets and ropes on the hooks.
- There are lots of balls in the room.
- The red wagon. (Mrs. Lewis prompts, "What is in the wagon, Ricky?" "Plastic bats, it's full of plastic bats," responds Ricky. Mrs. Lewis writes, "The red wagon is full of plastic bats.")
- The water bottles have green lids.

Mrs. Lewis records about a dozen sentences, and they read them together before closing the session.

"This morning, let's just have fun reading our great sentences." Mrs. Lewis turns to the flip chart and leads the students in choral reading. Then she smiles and says, "Now it's your turn to practice reading them by yourself and here they are." She gives each student a yellow page with the sentences numbered and printed in large font front and back and with the author's name printed under each sentence. She provides time for them to look at the 14 sentences (she included the model sentence word she created yesterday), share their comments, and ask questions about how it is set up. Their task is to find words they can read, find their sentence, and just have fun reading what they created.

Mrs. Lewis tells the students to find some space and practice their reading. As they find their space, she reminds them that they can use the chart or ask the author if they cannot read a word. The teacher walks around the classroom, listening to them read, discuss words, and talk about authorship. Occasionally, she sends someone to the chart to verify a word. Sometimes she pronounces a word for a student or asks someone to reread a sentence. Mrs. Lewis wants students to learn to use the chart routinely as an illustrated dictionary; she wants students to develop an awareness of when they do not know a word; and she is teaching good reference skills and use of the dictionary for looking up information when necessary.

Mrs. Lewis also encourages students to politely ask the author if they have trouble reading a word. She watches these interactions carefully because she wants to support students as they seek assistance from the author, but does not want students to become dependent or lazy as readers and learners.

Mrs. Lewis plans to extend the use of the picture word inductive model over the next several weeks. Tomorrow she plans to ask for sentences from other students and then to publish another page of sentences. Mrs. Lewis projects that several lessons will involve reading sentences, beginning to analyze them, identifying high-frequency words in the sentences—*the, is, in, there*—and mastering the words as sight words. By the time they finish their sentences, most students will be able to read them all.

Mrs. Lewis and her class of 25 students will continue to add words to their chart and sentences to their list, and the students will eventually classify the sentences and write paragraphs about what they found in the picture of the equipment room. As they work on reading, writing, spelling, phonics and phonemic awareness, structural analysis, and penmanship, they'll probably spend at least another two weeks on this picture chart. Nearly everyone will master 50 sight words and the most useful phonics generalizations in their words before they finish with the chart.

4

Designing Multidimensional Reading and Writing Instruction

The framework of the picture word inductive model allows us to teach several aspects of literacy simultaneously and to use multiple teaching and learning strategies. In this chapter, we look into the conceptual and operational framework of the PWIM and how it can be used to organize language arts instruction, address the movement between inductive activities and explicit instruction, and explain the emphasis on reading and writing informative prose.

Lessons taught using the picture word inductive model are dependent on and naturally blend the nature of instruction, content, and the roles of the students and teachers. The PWIM uses an integrated language arts approach to literacy: The teacher arranges instruction using the moves of the model, which is set up so that students work on developing skills and abilities in reading, writing, listening, and speaking as tools for thinking, learning, and sharing ideas. Learning how the written language works and using this information to read and write are the primary curricular and instructional emphases. In many ways, PWIM is a structured, formal approach to group language experiences, with metacognitive activities on how language works built into its sequence.

Using an Integrated Approach to Teaching and Learning

Using an integrated language arts approach to teaching and learning is not simply ideological, but is an instructional tool that saves time and builds learning skills that will last a lifetime for students. We need all modes of language and communication—listening, speaking, reading, writing, and all the connections among them—at work to help students come into literacy rapidly and infinitely. Multimodal activities, such as those within the PWIM, make instruction as productive as possible while saving time. For example, teachers and students save time because the language arts concepts addressed as Reading, Writing, Speaking, and Listening overlap in many curriculum documents. Consider the concept of the main idea, which may be listed under each heading:

- Reading: Reads to determine main idea.
- Writing: Writes with a clear subject and main idea.
- Speaking: Addresses the major point clearly.
- Listening: Listens to determine the main idea.

Working on these concepts simultaneously gives students more opportunities to master them at higher levels of performance. For example, if the instruction in comprehending the main idea of an informative piece and gaining conceptual control of how to figure out the main idea is followed by instruction in writing an informative paragraph that clearly announces the main idea and topic to the readers, the reading and writing connection eventually becomes visible to the students. Also, teachers gain better control over the language arts curriculum and have less stress about trying to cover the whole curriculum with independent lessons if they are able to present concepts simultaneously. And, if students can come to see the conceptual connections across the modes and mechanics of language, they can communicate far more skillfully and intentionally than most of us do—as readers, writers, speakers, and listeners. Think, again, about the main idea example:

- **Students as Readers.** If a student learns early and becomes increasingly skillful at gathering information and determining the main idea from prose (author-based meaning), that student is not only a good reader, but gains an advantage that is maintained throughout school and in most jobs and professions. Furthermore, if the student comes to see the writing craft in the prose being read—identifies the structure and content of the prose as the organization plus the ideas of another person who is trying to clearly communicate a main idea or message—then sentences, paragraphs, chapters, and books become exemplars or nonexemplars of writing with a clear subject or main idea.
- **Students as Writers.** If a student learns early and becomes increasingly skillful at gathering information from current knowledge, observations, and external resources, organizing this information, determining the main ideas to present to the readers in prose (author-based meaning and intent), that student is not only a good writer of informative prose, but gains an advantage that is maintained throughout school and in many jobs and professions.
- **Students as Speakers (participants in oral discourse).** If a student learns early and becomes increasingly skillful at gathering information from current knowledge and from additional resources, organizing this information, determining the main ideas to present to listeners (speaker-based meaning and intent), that student is not only a good speaker, discussant, conversationalist, but gains an advantage that is maintained throughout school and in most jobs and professions.
- **Students as Listeners.** If a student learns early and becomes increasingly skillful at gathering formation and determining the main idea from oral presentations, lectures, discussions, and conversations (speaker-based meaning), that student is not only a good listener, but gains an advantage that is maintained throughout school and in most jobs and professions.

The redundancy across the examples of possible student performance as readers, writers, speakers, and listeners is deliberate and emphasizes the conceptual connections and overlap across the modes.

Reinforcing the Mechanics of Language

The letters of the alphabet are part of a communications code in our society; this code can be interpreted and copied. Most students have seen words appear on the television screen, have seen many signs and labels, and have watched their parents or other caregivers write; therefore they do not come to us with an empty language bin. Many of our 5-year-old students come to school aware of the code (aware that letters mean something), so they come to us with some understanding of the mechanics of written language.

Similarities exist among the mechanics of language, especially among the areas of pronunciation, phonemic awareness, and spelling. Take a brief look at some of the similarities in teaching students how to learn to listen, speak, read, and write. Most students have the word *hat* in their listening and speaking vocabularies when they come to school; they already know what it means, what the phonemes /h/ /a/ /t/ in that order sound like, and most know how to pronounce the word. Formal literacy instruction builds on this knowledge. Through phonics, we teach students that *hat* is read /hat/; and through spelling we teach students that *hat* is spelled h-a-t.

In using the PWIM, we engage students in using all aspects of the language system and their prior knowledge. We want them to integrate their knowledge and use it to expedite their language learning. We anchor *hat* to a picture of a hat and connect the pronunciation to the word and to the spelling, with special attention to the order of the letters and to the formation of the letters. And we facilitate repetitions of these connections until mastery is attained.

Throughout the picture word inductive model, students experience the association of oral language with written language—they see it happening, see their words and ideas (words, phrases, and sentences) appear in print. The symbolic associations begin to be understood: pictures represent real things, words represent real things, sentences and longer examples of writing may represent stories and reality as seen by oneself and by others. The PWIM is designed so that students use the speaking, writing, and reading connection and the reading and writing connection continuously as they participate.

Focusing on Instructional Goals

While the picture word inductive model can be used to help students attain many of the language arts goals in our curriculum guidelines, the following instructional goals and accompanying student behaviors are constant for all learners:

- Building sight vocabulary as a base for reading and for learning phonics and spelling generalizations;
- Building confidence in one's ability to learn; and
- Learning how to inquire into language and using knowledge and skills to read and write and participate fully in education.

These instructional goals run under the surface of every lesson taught using the picture word inductive model. Remembering these goals as we observe students participate and respond shapes the use of the model with each group of students. Our cognitions about language, learning, teaching, and student performance guide our decision making within and through our implementation of the model. The information from this continuous scanning also supports other curriculum objectives we have for students and ones they have for themselves. Success with these instructional goals helps students to attain their goals—often stated simply and accurately:

- I want to be a good reader.
- I want to write.
- I am smart!

If the PWIM is a new strategy for you, use these diagnostic questions as you observe your students' behaviors:

- Is the PWIM helping individuals and the class as a whole add to their reading and writing vocabularies?
- Are they becoming more confident in themselves as learners?
- Are they able to articulate how language works with increasing clarity?
- Are they seeking and recognizing multiple answers from simple phonetic analyses, such as the letters *c* and *s* at times representing the same sounds (/c/ in *cents* and /s/ in *send*)?
- Are they recognizing that different informative paragraphs about their picture word chart having the same main idea?

Supporting Language Arts Goals and Objectives

Supporting language arts goals and objectives is built into the framework of the picture word inductive model, as it integrates reading, writing, speaking, and listening. The PWIM is designed to develop and support student growth in the following communication processes and specific skills:

- Reading—identifying sight words and performing phonetic analysis, structural analysis, contextual analysis, literal and inferential comprehension;
- Writing—recognizing the relationship between oral language and writing; sharing common meaning through words; composing sentences and paragraphs that convey ideas for ourselves and others; spelling; punctuation; letter formation; grammar and usage;
- Listening—including comprehension, identifying and discriminating details, gathering and organizing information; and as an expression of respect for others;
- Oral Language Development—sharing ideas clearly, responding orally to the ideas of others and blending ideas together, "publishing" orally;
- Mechanics—correctly forming and identifying the beginning and ending of words, sentences, paragraphs (and determining content

of paragraphs). Hundreds of repetitions are built into the PWIM for reading and spelling, but also for these mechanics of writing.

Gaining Literacy

Although it may not always be stated in our curriculum documents for language arts, one of our goals is to develop literate citizens. Literacy and its full expression as used in this book has no ceiling; it includes basic literacy, but goes far beyond. Literacy means using printed and written information to develop knowledge, to achieve goals, and to function in society. It is one of the ways people make sense of their world—both by acquiring information and ideas from others and through the process of expressing themselves. Therefore, literacy involves doing something, not just knowing something. Literate persons can understand and make sense of what others have written and can communicate effectively through writing.

Although reading and writing are given the major emphasis in this book, literacy has meaning beyond sheer competence in reading and writing. Literacy creates access to opportunities within schools and beyond, and the capability for full participation in a democratic society. Without skill in language use—both oral and written—a person cannot fulfill all the responsibilities of citizenship.

Supporting All Learning Opportunities

As words, sentences, and paragraphs are generated and analyzed, the teacher and students make continuous curriculum and instructional decisions about what becomes the focus of brief or long-term study. Along with objectives selected specifically by the teacher from one lesson or unit to the next, there is an unplanned instructional aspect to using the PWIM and a need for willingness to explore language through what students bring to the lesson.

In fact, much of the instruction about the mechanics of written language and the process of analysis could be described as informal or unplanned, but supported by continuous modeling and explanations. For example, a student identifies a *post office* in the picture and the teacher labels it. Another student volunteers *U.S. Post Office* and the teacher writes those words and asks what the *U.S.* means. After a discussion that includes ideas about abbreviations and the names of countries, the teacher adds *United States Post Office* to the list—giving three correct labels for the building in the picture. The students gain an overview of the complexities of language and communication, not counting the specifics of spelling, capitalization, and punctuation.

At any time during the lesson, even when the initial word list is being generated, the teacher can comment on compound words, punctuation marks, sentence structure, and whatever else seems appropriate. Through this informal format, this running dialog about how our language works, the teacher helps students to develop the foundation of cognizant control of language and of standard written communication. From the first lesson with the model, students are invited and expected to comment on what they see in the words or sentences. Through this process they are developing hypotheses about clues and general rules on how our language works. I owe a tremendous conceptual debt to the work of Stauffer (1969) for helping me learn to think about providing instruction as part of building cognition even with the simplest language arts tasks.

The teacher's attitude when sharing what is noticed about the words is critical. Some teachers call their students detectives, explorers, or investigators. These teachers want their students to enjoy inquiring into language and how it works. They want the students to inquire individually and as partners—both with the teacher and with other students. Eventually, much of the content of this informal instruction or commentary shows up as attributes in the word groups and categories that students form and shows up in their independent reading and writing.

In some ways, the traditional "why" questions of early childhood are reversed in many teacher and student interactions, for when statements or assertions are made about language, the teacher will often ask "why do you say that?" or "show us what you mean," or "show us and explain how that works." Most students come to provide evidence and examples automatically and are less conditioned to the teacher as questioner and to themselves as seekers of the one right answer.

Moving Between Inductive Activities and Explicit Instruction

The PWIM units include inductive activities and explicit instruction. You may opt for explicit instruction on any aspect of the language system you select, that you feel students are ready to move forward to, or that they are having difficulty with. For example, explicit instruction may be used for developing skills in phonics, structural analysis, and contextual analysis applications; explaining and modeling reading comprehension processes, such as determining the main idea; and explaining and modeling any aspect of the writing craft. If you are not familiar with explicit instruction, see Appendix 1; refer to Appendix 2 for information related to the concept attainment model for explicit instruction.

Using the words generated by the students, lesson segments can be designed to work on phonetic analysis (e.g., boy, book, board—all begin with b; as in the list created by Mrs. Frazier's students) or on phonemic awareness (understanding that spoken words are made of speech sounds that are represented by one or more letters). You can also select words for teaching structural analysis (determining word meaning or pronunciation from analyzing the word parts). For lesson examples, see Graves (1992, pp. 117–121); Nagy, Winsor, Osborn, and O'Flahavan 1994); and Graves, Watts, and Graves (1994, pp. 124–127).

For lessons in phonetic analysis, look at the word list for words that exhibit phonics or spelling patterns you have been working on with your students (e.g., begin with the same consonant, end with the same consonant, or rhyme). I strongly recommend building on simple rhyming patterns for three interrelated reasons: they are easy to learn; they can be used to build reading and writing vocabulary rapidly, providing a base for practicing word recognition skills being acquired and common spelling patterns and letter order; and students tend to perceive language patterns easily (Adams, 1990; Goswami & Bryant 1990, 1992; Treiman 1992). When working with beginning readers, look for rhyming words in the word list.

You can move from the rhyming words to developing word families or patterns by using onsets and rimes. Onsets are the initial part of the word, such as /f/ in fan and the /pl/ in plan and the rime is the part of the word that rhymes in the pattern. The onset is a consonant or consonant cluster; the rime is the pattern's vowel and any consonants following it. The use of onsets and rimes are also known as using word families (e.g., at, bat, cat, that), phonograms, or graphemic bases (-at) and are part of decoding words by analogy.

For lessons in structural analysis—using word parts to determine the meaning and pronunciation of words—look for examples of suffixes, prefixes, and compound words in the word list. Nagy and Anderson (1984) estimate that as many as 60 percent of English words have meanings that can be predicted from the meanings of their parts (Nagy, Winsor, Osborn, & O'Flahavan, 1994). The words that have the five most common suffixes (-s, -ed, -ing, -ly, and -er) are useful in building your students' vocabulary. Compound words also offer a powerful scaffold for building reading vocabulary.

While classifying words, many students form groups using structural analysis. For example, students often use the suffix -s to make a plural noun (e.g., girls, books, students) and identify the group as meaning more than one. Or they will recognize compound words (e.g., basketball, baseball, outside, railroad) as two words that make one word. Identifying additional words for these categories and using explicit instruction will help students learn how to use structural analysis to determine word meaning and to stretch their beginning reading, writing, and spelling skills.

What is explicit instruction in comprehension and composition? It is structured inquiry in action, a teacher-directed approach that can be used to teach comprehension and composition strategies. Explicit instruction includes teacher modeling and explanation, guided practice during which teachers gradually give students more responsibility for task completion and independent practice, and applications of the reading or writing strategy in real situations (Fielding & Pearson, 1994).

Strategy instruction in composing and comprehending all the moves of prose occurs throughout the year in classrooms where teachers use the PWIM. Strategy instruction was modeled by Ms. Frazier's students when they classified a group of words by topic: words that identified people (e.g., boy, girl, child, children, people, persons) when we don't know or use their personal names. Strategy instruction also occurred when Ms. Frazier talked to her students about how she put together a paragraph using one of their suggested titles and one of their groups of sentences. The continuous discussion and dialog about how to share one's ideas using a word label, a sentence, or a paragraph is part of almost every PWIM lesson. Explicit modeling is used to show how ideas become words, sentences, and paragraphs, and is part of the year-long instruction on writing.

Balancing Learning with Nonfiction

The picture word inductive model focuses on reading and writing non-fiction prose instead of fiction or narrative stories. The materials used—pictures with familiar items or realistic photographs, informative trade books, paragraphs written by the teacher—and the group instruction concentrate on reading and composing informative prose. Of course, the PWIM lessons can be focused on learning to read and write fiction or nonfiction because the phonetic analysis, structural analysis, sight words, high-frequency words, mechanics, and syntax are the same. I sharply focus whole-class work—with the pictures, the group lessons, and the books used in a PWIM unit—on nonfiction, informative and expository prose, for several reasons:

• Much of the writing in kindergarten through 3rd grade is personal narrative and journal writing; such writing is good, appropriate, and I believe in it. At the same time, I desire a balance between writing fiction and nonfiction, and I believe instruction in the primary grades should include how to share and support ideas when writing informative prose.

• Many of the books that teachers read aloud to kindergartners through 8th graders are fiction. I have known few teachers who regularly read and share excellent examples of high-quality nonfiction. Early sharing through oral reading, which also functions to model what is pleasurable and useful, is incredibly powerful.

• Exposition is dominant in textbooks, especially in those geared for beyond the 4th grade. I am concerned about student comprehension of informative prose, and believe that students need to be better prepared to handle it. We can help students comprehend informative prose more efficiently if they generate and classify sentences and participate in building informative paragraphs that become part of their reading material.

• The work of students in higher grades, and even the work of adults in professional settings, indicate that they need work in writing clear, accurate, well-grounded informative pieces. Thus, I shape and use the PWIM to provide balance and early practice on gathering, organizing, summarizing, and interpreting information as a reader and a writer. These aspects of literacy and the mode of thinking as gatherer and sharer of information are important to success in school, out of school, and as a community citizen.

• Observational skills and research skills are developed through the use of photographs and pictures, for students are taught to base what they say and write on evidence in the pictures.

For additional instructional suggestions and rationale for teaching primary grade students to write and read informative prose, see especially Moss, Leone, and Dipillo, 1997. For an extended discussion of the similarities in student performance of native English and native Spanish speakers in reading and writing fiction and nonfiction see Langer, Bartolome, Vasquez, and Lucas, 1990.

▼   ▼   ▼

Even those students who come to us without literacy and learning goals wish to become fuller participants in the language world when immersed in a productive and caring, literacy-rich instructional environment for 20 or more hours a week. Teachers working with language impoverished students have a greater professional burden and a more complex challenge than the rest of us. Through the learning environment they create and the literacy instruction they provide, these educators open the windows of the world for their students. They are in a position to help students desire an expanded world, obtain greater access to opportunities, and have more choices in life.

Using an integrated approach to teaching language arts, keeping language learning goals and student learning behaviors constantly in mind, and providing a better balance between nonfiction and fiction in our written and unwritten curriculum help us to offer students a multidimensionl approach to learning to read and write. Within each unit of the PWIM, familiar or realistic pictures are used to elicit words, sentences and a general discussion of the scene. Teachers model writing informative sentences and paragraphs and provide opportunities for students to write informative sentences and paragraphs.

As for materials to read aloud, I encourage teachers to select well-written, informative trade books to support the topics or events related to the picture and to skills being taught. Whether it turns out that the emphasis on fiction and personal narrative dominant in so many primary grade language arts programs has hindered the achievement of young males in the literacy curriculum (Millard, 1997), a better balance in modeling and producing fiction and nonfiction seems like a healthy approach for both males and females. (See Appendix 3 for additional comments on vocabulary development and Appendix 4 for a brief rationale for using opportunities to read aloud informative prose.)

5

Getting Started in Your Classroom or School

If you decide to try the PWIM, use the suggestions in this chapter to support your effort. I've included general advice about learning a new teaching strategy, the specifics of selecting and using pictures, establishing the learning community, teaching students the moves of the model, and selecting content for instruction. The chapter closes with a list of teaching tips and a few of the reasons I've found the PWIM so useful.

My best advice: If the picture word inductive model appeals to you, if you think it might help your students to move forward in literacy, give it a try. Whether I'm standing in front of an audience, working with a staff over time, or writing this book, I'm aware that I cannot teach you to be highly skilled in using any strategy or curriculum device. You have to teach yourself by using the strategy, watching what happens for students, and reflecting on the experience. I can provide information, give examples or scenarios of what the strategy looks like in action, explain how to organize peer support and peer coaching, and offer personal support and encouragement.

Offering support and facilitating implementation through print is difficult: It's hard to support someone learning a new teaching strategy by writing about how to do it, even if I have a whole book in which to do it. I can describe the general language arts goals that are similar across classrooms, I can describe the syntax of the model—its sequence and the moves you make to get the students from one stage to the next. But the magic—the reason for using the PWIM—occurs in specific contexts with students, teachers, pictures, and content. It's difficult to capture the richness and variability of teacher and student responses, the curriculum breadth of what is generated, and the constant switching between formal and informal (unplanned) teaching that occurs during teacher and student interactions. Despite my use of scenarios, it's difficult to illustrate the range of moves available during instruction, thereby making it difficult to support you in specific classroom circumstances. You may find support from a partner, especially if you have already experienced peer coaching. It may be limp support, but trust yourself and your students. The PWIM is productive and fun.

Do not rush the teaching and learning process, or much of the multidimensional, continuous assessment qualities of the PWIM lessons will be lost. Observe what your students produce, and listen to what they can articulate about what they see. Build sight vocabulary, work on useful phonics generalizations and phonemic awareness and spelling patterns, work on structural analysis, work on modeling and writing informative prose, work on reading informative prose. Teach your students how to inquire into language, how to break the code and to move forward in language literacy.

Selecting and Using Pictures

The pictures are the basic materials for the PWIM. The right pictures are tangible, concrete, and attractive, and they provide an excellent stimulus for common work in language development.

With preschool, kindergarten, and 1st grade students, use large

pictures of scenes that are somewhat familiar and include several representations or objects that are familiar to most students: pictures with
children and animals, inside or outside. Using pictures or photographs
that are easily understandable and accessible to your students helps
them to be immediately and personally successful in visually reading
the picture—shaking words out of the picture (visually "reading" it)
and generating the word list. The word list forms part of the language
curriculum for at least a week and gives the students ownership of their
learning.

Using real pictures (photographs or posters of real scenes or scenes
that students can easily relate to) has many advantages. Just by using
real pictures, you can help students develop their skills in beginning
research and using their observation skills to base what they say and
write on evidence. In most primary schools, students have much more
experience with fiction and narrative writing than with nonfiction and
the development of informative, high-quality exposition. The PWIM
can be used to offer a more balanced approach in teaching written communication by helping students to learn to use their observational
skills as a source of information when writing. In general, using observation skills as a source of information for writing is a far underused
resource, but those skills are always available and waiting to be tapped
by us and by our students. And, the concrete and common stimuli of the
picture and the chart allows the teacher wonderful specificity and common examples to use in discussions about writing informative sentences
and paragraphs and gives ample opportunities for metacognitive activities on forming and shaping ideas.

Whatever the age of the students or the nature of the class, the pictures promote the expansion of students' reading and writing vocabularies, the mechanics of phonics and spelling and language usage, and
the use of observation in providing content and evidence in oral and
written discourse.

On Finding Pictures

Photographs are great! Sources may include calendars, posters, book companies, stores, old magazines such as *Instructor* and *Life*, newspapers, and enlarged photographs. You may find public libraries, bookstores, and card shops getting rid of (culling their files or selling for a drastically reduced price) picture photographs of an area or of some topic relevant to your curriculum. Ask parents and other caregivers to keep their eyes open for appropriate posters and photographs.

For prekindergarten through 1st grade (maybe even 2nd grade), 12 good pictures are all you will need for a school year. In fact, for most kindergarten and 1st grade classes, six or eight good pictures may be enough because of the time needed to build sight vocabulary; to see and learn the generalizations about how letters and words work in each set of words generated for a single chart; and to read, write, and play with the language the students have generated around the picture. For some 2nd grade classes and for 3rd grade classes, choose 15–20 pictures. Consider laminating the pictures for reuse.

On Interrelating the Curriculum

Pictures can be a vehicle for interdisciplinary instruction. At the end of 2nd grade or the beginning of 3rd grade, the pictures and the PWIM units can begin to serve other disciplines along with language arts. The pictures and photographs that you select can support social studies and science concepts, can be used to open an area of study, and can become a focal point for discussions, examples, and the gathering of additional information as students explore a domain or subject.

For social studies, pictures of the neighborhood, the community, the town, or events may help to simultaneously anchor and expand students' explorations of these settings. In science, pictures of animals in their usual environments (near a doghouse, in a rain forest, or in the ocean), or pictures of plants (on a window sill, in the desert, or in the ocean), or photographs of businesses and services (of a dairy, of workers in a commercial kitchen, or of a dental hygienist at work) may stimulate and support discussion. The list of possibilities is as extensive as the concepts and topics within the curriculum area.

Through the pictures selected by the teacher, students navigate the curriculum, using the pictures as a source for in-depth study and for practice in gathering evidence to support assertions and generalizations.

Developing the Learning Community

For students to fully participate in the PWIM, they need to learn the basic routines and behaviors appropriate to the learning environment (especially social expectations). These routines and expectations are integral to the PWIM and are necessary for the teacher to maintain focus and sanity, and for the students to experience the appropriate pace and mix of group and individual instruction.

Introducing the PWIM Routines

When the picture word inductive model is first used, you need to help students learn the format and sequence of the model and the social routines that facilitate lots of children working and learning together. You need to teach students how to participate in a group—teaching them explicitly by explaining and demonstrating or by role-playing the moves, or by rehearsing specific actions with a small group of students and then presenting the results to the class. For example, students may need explanations and demonstrations of any one or all of the following actions:

• Studying each new picture as it goes up so they will be ready to contribute (some teachers put the picture up a day before they are ready to "shake" the first set of words from it);

• Knowing the signal for coming efficiently to their space near the picture word chart (many teachers use the PWIM early in the day, right after their morning routine);

• Speaking loudly enough to be heard by their classmates and the teacher;

  • Learning to listen to each other;
  • Learning to raise their hands to signal for attention;
  • Learning to listen and "hold their thoughts" while waiting;
  • Reading silently and aloud;
  • Thinking silently;
  • Responding appropriately to the task at hand;
  • Keeping up with their word cards;

  • Sharing space at the picture word chart, especially the first few days of a new chart when they are practicing their reading; and

  • Finding and sharing work space around the room when they are classifying words and sentences or putting sentences together.

Teaching Silent Reading

Teaching students to read words silently when using the PWIM is very important to the success of the model and the students. Work toward 100 percent silent reading—when you request it. Silent reading is important in helping students to build sight vocabulary and providing them with practice in applying phonics skills. If all students are to have ample opportunities for the numbers of rehearsals and repetitions of words and phrases needed for rapid movement of the words on the chart to their reading and writing vocabularies (with the automaticity of sight words), they will need to learn "to read it in your mind but not to say it out loud." Silent reading of the words provides many opportunities for practice and mental rehearsal. You may want to demonstrate silent reading in contrast to various forms of oral reading (whispering, normal tone of voice for group size, shouting); ham it up if that works for you and with your students.

There is a balance between oral reading and silent reading throughout the sequence of lessons that is difficult for me to explain and difficult for you to understand until you have used the PWIM. At times you want students so engaged in reading the words orally that they are shouting; at other times, you want them engaged in studying and reading a word or all the words silently.

Many of the behaviors and social skills required for the successful use of the PWIM are also needed for participating in groups and classroom activities and are part of daily classroom management. With students, especially those in kindergarten through 2nd grade, some of these skills and expected behaviors may need to be taught or reinforced. As always, use your common sense and your sense of humor. Take some time modeling and explaining behaviors the first few times you use the PWIM—young students particularly enjoy humor and skits when their teacher demonstrates appropriate and inappropriate behaviors. Many of these demonstrations and initial learning experiences can be grand fun for you and your students.

Setting the Social Climate and Lesson Pace

Part of what we strive for with this teaching model is helping students to learn that they are responsible for thinking things through and for applying what they are learning. For this to occur, students need time to think, listen, and build on ideas and on things they've learned from previous lessons. Teachers often find they need to move the lessons more slowly than they are accustomed to, especially the first time or two through the model. From the beginning, try to consciously balance thinking time and a cheerful learning pace. The PWIM is not the total language arts program, therefore, short intense lessons from 20 to 30 minutes are often best for students up through 2nd grade.

From the first use of the PWIM, the teacher will model providing thinking time and being patient when listening to others. Teachers find that even with 4-year-old students they can say, "Hold on, we need to make sure everyone has time to think and share." It isn't necessary, however, to insist that every student volunteer a word for the chart. You may invite anyone who has not contributed a word or comment to the day's lesson to do so and then say, "maybe you'll have something for us later." Some students are simply shy, and some students have already—even at 5 years old—begun to think they are not star learners, not as smart as their classmates, or that their comments or answers are not as welcome as those of others. When you feel this may be the case—despite your speculation about its origin (circumstances at home, overcrowded daycare centers, the student's personality)—you want to address it in as many ways as possible to help these students reestablish their faith in their natural learning ability.

Both group and individualized instruction occur throughout the PWIM; however, all students participate in all the phases of the model at the same time. When words are being chosen for the lessons, you want everyone attending the event; for example, all students are seated near the picture when words are being shaken out. When it's time to practice reading and matching words, everyone practices reading. When it's time to classify, everyone classifies: from the student who puts a set of word cards together because they all have one word, to the student who groups *apples*, *trees*, and *leaves* together because they all mean "some, not one," to the student who groups *ladder*, *leaves*, and *little* together because they "all sound alike at the first, they all begin with an *l* and it looks like a [number] 1."

A wide range of accurate responses, such as those described, is common and is one of the curriculum advantages of the picture word inductive model: there is no curriculum or academic limit on what students can learn about language and how it works. Anything they can see, articulate, or verify can become content for individual and group instruction.

Another general curriculum and instructional advantage is the opportunity for constant assessment of progress. As much of what is generated by students is visible and there is time to listen and think built into the model, constant diagnosis of student progress in language arts becomes a less-stressful task than it usually is for most primary teachers. Results are immediately used for modulations in the next example or set of examples provided, the next question asked, or the next lesson planned.

The development of each group into a cooperative learning community inquiring into reading, writing, and their own thought processes is supported not only by the research on cooperative learning for social benefits and improvements in student achievement (Johnson & Johnson, 1989; Sharan, 1990; Slavin, 1995), but also by the social context of reading and writing as communication (Bloome, 1987; Myers, 1992; Shanahan, 1990; Tierney & Shanahan, 1991) and by the sociocognitive nature of reading and writing, that is, "that language learning is ultimately an interactive process, that cognitive factors are influenced by context, and that they, in turn, affect the meanings that are produced" (Langer, 1986). Much of language and language learning is about learning to communicate.

The PWIM can be used for small group instruction and for tutorial sessions, but it was designed primarily as a productive model for whole class instruction in beginning reading and writing. I describe the PWIM as a productive model because it helps the teacher to develop and to continually diagnose students' language skills.

Identifying Content for Instruction

Content for instruction is largely generated by the students, as prompted by the teacher's selection of the picture. Although the picture motivates students and initially drives instruction, the teacher selects the picture, can influence the direction of the lesson depending on her assessment of student needs, and can focus instruction on many different areas of language development.

The Word List

Students volunteer the words for study. While the teacher can always add words, at least 95 percent of the words should come from the students—whether the words are from their spoken vocabulary or from their investigations. The formality and extent of these investigations range from a thorough exploration of the picture, to discussions with other students, to adding words they find from reading picture books or informative trade books, or to having books and excerpts read to them.

How many words do you write on the chart? There's no magic number. Many teachers who are skilled in using the PWIM in kindergarten and 1st grade stop at the first round (the first time words are shaken from a picture) when the students have generated around 30 words. If students generate only 15 words, go with 15 for the first sequence of lessons. Use your judgment, and keep the lesson moving briskly while providing adequate thinking time.

"Shaking the words from the picture" is a celebration of how much your students already know about symbols, language, and communication. You want them to feel this celebration and to feel that they are participating in shaping their education.

Using the Chart

The picture word chart serves as an illustrated dictionary, as a focal point for discussion, as a base of evidence for informative writing, and as a vehicle to support interrelated curriculum work. As an illustrated dictionary, post the picture word chart where students can use it to support their reading, their writing, and their independence as learners. Until the words are part of the student's sight vocabulary, they are anchored in their representations on the picture chart.

The picture word chart can be titled and retitled. Beginning with kindergartners, the teacher helps students to think about which title is most comprehensive, which title would be most interesting to one audience or another, and which suggested titles are good announcements of what we wish to share with our readers. When writing a paragraph, or creating a title, help students to focus on the essence of communication: What do we want to say to our readers? to ourselves?

We make explicit the reading and writing connection by having students think about what they want to share, what they most want the reader to know, how they can help the reader to get this information, and, finally, to decide if we as writers shared what we wanted to share, beginning with the title and ending with the last sentence.

Curriculum Decisions

When using the PWIM, decisions about what to emphasize and teach to mastery depends on which aspects of the curriculum you wish to pursue with your students and what is conceptually accessible to them as language learners. The teacher—while still the obvious adult authority, instructional leader, and curriculum expert—does not know which specific language concepts will be emphasized until the students generate the words.

To try the PWIM, you need to trust yourself and your students. You will not know which sight words, which aspects of constructing meaning, which phonics generalizations or aspects of phonemic awareness, which aspects of structural analysis (e.g., compound words, inflected endings, plurals, contractions), spelling (e.g., final -e rule, doubling the final consonant, capital letters for proper nouns), and punctuation (e.g., hyphens, apostrophes, terminal marks) will be possible content for lessons—until the words are shaken out of the picture; until additional words are gathered; until the sentences are generated. Fortunately, in most word and phrase lists of 25 to 35 items and lists of 15 to 25 sentences, there are almost unlimited language arts objectives available for instruction.

As words, sentences, and paragraphs are generated and analyzed, the teacher and students make decisions about what will be studied. For example, Mrs. Lewis did not know for certain her 1st graders would generate a word list that included so many words with the initial consonant *b*; or several rhyming words that facilitated the exploration of onsets and rimes; or several compound words, thus providing content for a productive exploration of structural analysis. In Chapter 1, Ms. Tayloe was not certain that her kindergartners would generate a list with singular and plural words; or so many words with identical consonants side by side, forming two-syllable words, thus providing content for exploring that particularly rich phonics and spelling generalization. The 2nd graders in Chapter 1 may have surprised Mrs. Frazier by generating different words to represent people and dictating sentences that related to student learning.

Part of the instruction about the mechanics of written language and the process of analysis is informally embedded in the lessons, and the modeling and explanations and dialog about how language works are continuous. By "informal," I mean that the teacher did not plan to introduce or teach that concept; it surfaced during the lesson and was introduced or extended on the spot. For example, in the 1st grade scenario, when a student suggested adding *tooks* and *shooks* to the list of /o͝o/ words, Mrs. Lewis introduced into the lesson the printed and written standard English words *take* and *shake*. Another example of this informal learning occurred when a student suggested adding *middle* and *riddle* to the category with *little*—Mrs. Lewis immediately went to work on pronunciation differences between /t/ and /d/ and on rhyming words.

From the first lesson with the model, students are invited and expected to comment on what they see in the words or sentences: they are developing clues and general rules about how our language works. Teaching them to ground the comments they make in evidence helps us to understand how they are thinking and is part of our continual diagnosis into their progress as language learners and into where we can take them next. When statements or assertions are made about language, the teacher will often ask the student to explain the idea; eventually, most students learn to automatically provide evidence and examples.

If you are a new teacher or if you have concerns about what to aim for or which available objectives may be most important for lesson content, you can use any good language arts or reading textbook as a guide, teacher's manuals that accompany basal systems, and in some places, district curriculum guides. So, look to your favorite resources.

If you wish to add a few resources to your classroom or school collection, a particularly comprehensive reading textbook with many charts and ample discussion for teaching phonics and structural analysis, building vocabulary, and developing reading comprehension is *Creating Reading Instruction for All Children* by Thomas G. Gunning (1996). For more information and ideas about using the reading and writing connection, *Reading Writing Connections: From Theory to Practice* by Mary F. Heller (1991) is a beautifully articulated resource. Also, classic articles such as Clymer's (1996/1963) "The Utility of Phonic Generalizations in the Primary Grades" are especially valuable in deciding which phonic categories are most useful and reliable.

Teaching Tips

Using the 10 moves that make up the general sequence of the PWIM, I have listed a few teaching tips. Some of these tips may seem obvious. However, I've learned them from watching highly skilled teachers use the model, seeing students struggle unnecessarily, or experiencing some part of teaching and learning the hard way. While many of these tips are applicable to using the PWIM with any group size, I write them with whole-class instruction in mind.

1. Tips for selecting a picture

• The richer the content of the picture, the more opportunities for language development and expansion. For example, a beautiful photograph of a child sitting alone on a bench may not generate many words, but a photograph that includes a child, puppies, trees, and flowers is likely to generate many words. Select pictures you think your students can relate to.

- The larger the picture the better (24" x 30" is great).
- If you find a great picture that you think will evoke many words and ideas from your students, go ahead and laminate it to use again next year. Laminating allows you to erase or make changes in the lines you draw from the picture to the phrase or word.
- As you pin or tape the picture to the background paper, ensure the paper extends about three feet beyond the picture on all sides. I still make mistakes in not allowing myself enough good writing space when students generate more words than I anticipate. White or light-color paper makes an easy-to-read background.
- When you place the picture on the board or wall, place it at eye level for your students to aid their exploration and gathering of evidence.

2. Tips for identifying items and ideas

- The first round or two of identifying items in the picture needs to be relatively fast-paced with clear, easy matches between the items and the labels (whether a word or phrase).
- If you are concerned about a student not participating from shyness or lack of language, have an impromptu individual discussion with that student. Help the student think about what is in the picture.
- Focus first on recording words and identifying phrases about the picture. If a student volunteers a sentence, you may simply write the key words on the chart. For example, write *brown truck*, instead of "I see a brown truck in the picture."
- If a students volunteers a particularly descriptive sentence, you can always comment on it and save it by jotting it down in your notebook. If the sentence is "That brown truck is a delivery truck because it has UPS on it," use any or all of the following labels identified by you or the student: *brown truck*, *delivery truck*, *brown delivery truck*, or *UPS truck*.

3. Tips for labeling the picture

• Write the words in large enough print so that the student who is the greatest distance from the chart will be able to read them clearly and easily. Generally, this means "the tall letters" need to be about three or four inches high. (A blunt tip magic marker is great!)

• Write the words horizontally. If you write at a slant, you may find some of your kindergartners writing the word at the same slant.

• With young children who are still learning letter recognition and letter formation, watch where you stand as you see, say, and spell each word.

• Draw two or more lines when students offer a label that represents more than one item, for example, *trees*.

• If students provide several accurate labels for the same item, write all labels on the chart; for example, *brown truck, delivery truck, UPS truck.*

• If students give you an abstract description such as "happy boy," ask them for their evidence to help reinforce observation and reference skills.

• If you are not certain about the correct spelling of a word, say so, and develop a common signal you and the students can use to indicate this uncertainty, such as a question mark. You may choose to check the spelling during the lesson or to check it later and report to students at the beginning of the next lesson. Another option is to have a brief discussion with them about why this word still gives you problems, or explain that it was a new word for you and you spelled it phonetically. When students are older or are experienced with the model, you can have them check the correct spelling of the word for homework or classwork.

4. Tips for reading and reviewing the picture word chart

• The first few days of a new chart, or every day depending on the circumstances, lead the students in reading all the words. You want students to hear the words pronounced correctly many times, and to have extensive practice reading the words aloud and silently, as a group and independently.

• Especially with a new chart or when teaching a class new to the PWIM, put strips of tape on the floor to identify a space for each student to sit and to see the chart.

• The first few days of a new chart, lead them in spelling the words. You want students to hear the words spelled correctly many times and to participate in spelling the words correctly. After a few days, you may want to target words to spell that will be mastered first for reading and writing.

• Teach students how to check their reading by using the word chart—an activity that is part of early instruction in reference skills.

• Teach students how to read the words on the chart silently.

• Select words, sound and symbol relationships, or phonics generalizations to address informally or to teach explicitly—selection can occur at any time.

5. Tips for reading and classifying the words

• Each student needs a word envelope or word bank and needs to be responsible for a personal set of word cards.

• The first day or two of reading the words using the chart should be an exciting event for younger students and should not be rushed. Teach them how to share space at the chart and facilitate their exploration of the picture and the model. Listen for and record words that are difficult for several students.

• The teacher needs a large set of the word cards for group instruction and demonstrations. A large pocket chart helps to align words and sentences so students can see patterns that are present in groups of words or sentences.

• Ensure that the class generates enough words to classify. It's difficult to put an exact number on this, but it's possible to begin with from

10 to 15 words. With some groups of students, you may wish to give students a few words at a time.

• As you listen to students read the words and form word groups, refer them to the chart if a word is not in their sight vocabulary and they cannot figure it out. Using the chart helps them to learn to gather information, to develop problem-solving skills, and to develop reference skills.

• Have students work independently to classify the words several times to push them into observing and identifying details.

• You can select any category, group of words, or group of sentences for explicit instruction or for concept attainment lessons to drive for class mastery of useful concepts or generalizations.

6. Tips for reading and reviewing the picture word chart

• Select words of common difficulty for group instruction.

• Identify certain common concepts in the words to emphasize with the class as a whole. Pull out any useful group for explicit instruction. Brief explicit instruction episodes throughout the PWIM are used to support mastery of selected concepts and provide demonstrations of language analysis.

7. Tips for adding words

• The teacher may add a word to the picture word chart at any time, for either word analysis (phonetic analysis or structural analysis) or for content purposes (some important item or action in the picture).

• Provide opportunities for students to add new words as they spend more time with the picture and more time reading informative books related to the content. Two relevant management tips: you may want to write these new words with a different color magic marker and you need to add the words to each student's set.

• Adding words can be a stimulus for searching through books.

• Use a word wall or flip chart for the words that are collected by students as they pursue various sound and symbol applications, structural similarities (e.g., different ways plurals are formed), or content groups (e.g., all different labels for "people when we do not know their names," or for "other names we call people we know, like Grandad"). Many of these words will not belong on the picture word chart but are needed to help students apply the concepts being taught through the PWIM.

8. Tips for creating titles

• Picture word charts can be titled simply using the picture as the information base.

• Lead students to think about the "evidence" and information in their chart and about what they want to "announce" first to the reader.

• Picture word charts can be titled more than one time, just put a sentence strip over the first title.

• Lead the development of collaborative sentences using words students have classified by content (e.g., the group labeled by a student in Mrs. Frazier's classroom as "all names for humans" or the group in Mrs. Lewis's class labeled as "all the kinds of balls in the storage room").

• After sentences have been generated, read, and classified, select appropriate categories for developing collaborative paragraphs (e.g, a paragraph about the topic of students wearing uniforms).

• Read to students the titles and first paragraphs or pages from well-written informative books. Reading aloud these sections may take only five minutes, but the experience can be instructionally rich as the teacher is able to (1) provide models of accurate titles for informative prose selections; (2) ensure that students hear good nonfiction prose read well; (3) help students to develop a sense of the rhythms of the English language; (4) advertise books and encourage students to read about a particular subject; (5) demonstrate the amount of information available in books written at a range of ability levels, from picture books to adult nonfiction; and (6) provide students with another opportunity to learn about a concept being taught in science, social studies, or mathematics. Depending on the picture, the informative books can be used for interdisciplinary instruction.

9. Tips for generating sentences and paragraphs

• Build on what students already know and bring to the learning experience; model thinking aloud and appropriate discussions; help students to expand their knowledge base about how language works.

• As with the word cards, students need copies of everyone's sentences. With some groups, you may choose to work with a few sentences at a time. Especially with kindergarten and 1st graders, publishing sentences makes a grand publishing and sharing event.

• Reading aloud titles and paragraphs from informative trade books is useful throughout the time students are working on moves 7–10, but especially when working on generating sentences, paragraphs, and titles.

• Encourage students to write additional sentences and paragraphs in their journals.

• Use student sentences and paragraphs to create books they can read easily. Students can illustrate their sentences in a class book.

10. Tips for reading and reviewing sentences and paragraphs

• Remember that the goal is for everyone to learn to read the sentences and paragraphs fluently.

• Listen and look for high-frequency words that need to be mastered rapidly, through word card games and drill if necessary, along with demonstrations of analysis of their characteristics or differences (e.g., *the, they, them, their; it, is, in*).

• Encourage students to find pictures in magazines or newspapers that relate to the class picture word chart and to create their own related independent picture word charts. This can be additional language arts work, part of work in other subject areas, or work with parents and caregivers.

Management and Assessment Reminders

It's useful to occasionally have additional help. Possible avenues include an upper-grade group as buddies for your students and parent or community volunteers. These support persons can do everything from writing or printing and cutting word cards to checking the number of words students have mastered as sight words.

Despite group and individual diagnosis being continuous when using the PWIM, you may also use formal assessment measures for additional diagnostic data. Each lesson loop (day) provides data for a range of options in that lesson or for the next day's lesson. Keeping a notebook handy for notes on common needs, future steps, and particular aspects of language confusion by individual students, is useful. If you wish, you may use general assessment instruments like the *Names Test* (see Duffelmeyer, Merkley, Fyfe, & Kruse, 1994) or *Emergent Literacy Survey/K–2* (Pikulski, 1997), or any general phonics assessment instrument that provides results by sound and symbol, thus providing additional data for making decisions about which phonics elements to focus on for whole class or small group instruction.

The PWIM as a Multipurpose Teaching Strategy

In working with school faculties and in teaching staff development courses, I have a slogan: "Let's make it fun and productive!" The *it* is the learning experience of participating in the year's collective work or the course. Although we do not always succeed, the slogan represents a social climate and achievement goal that is part of my teaching stance. I feel the same way about classroom instruction. The cognitive work of learning to read and write can be fun. Language learning can be fun. And, instruction in reading and writing needs to engage students and needs to be productive work for both students and teachers.

I enjoy using the PWIM and helping others to use it with their students because it's fun. Generally, students and teachers enjoy language learning with the picture word inductive model. And, balancing the multiple demands of classroom curriculum manager, I can make it serve many curriculum objectives and use it to apply what I know about good learning theory.

For language arts curriculum, the PWIM can be focused on building sight vocabulary, on letter and sound relationships, on phonetic and structural analysis, on spelling, on reading comprehension, on writing (including composition, mechanics, and penmanship), and on reference skills. The wonderful thing about the PWIM is that students generate part of the curriculum: It's their words, their phrases, their sentences, and their paragraphs that form the content of picture word inductive lessons. PWIM also allows us to apply good learning theories from a variety of perspectives:

• Repetition and presentation of words on the picture word chart convert the words into sight words for most students.

• Repetition, presentation, and discussion of the formation of letters and the sounds they represent result in language tools for students' reading and writing (and spelling).

• Analysis and application of phonetic and structural generalizations help students to acquire those patterns.

• Continuous opportunities exist for explicit instruction in reading comprehension and in composing, including modeling of the metacognitive processes involved in skill areas (e.g., spelling and pronunciation) and modeling the more comprehensive language processes (e.g., organizing an informative paragraph for a designated audience; determining importance; making and checking predictions in reading).

• Individual, small-group, and large-group activities are part of the PWIM structure.

• Opportunities are available for using the social setting to develop understanding and use of multiple perspectives, to apply listening and discussion skills, and to gather information from multiple sources.

• Multiple opportunities are available for students to apply the language concepts they are learning.

For organizing learning experiences and the school day, the PWIM can be allotted any length of time, depending on the number of concepts being taught or reinforced. And, thinking about the need to integrate instruction because of the limited amount of instructional time available, the PWIM can be used for teaching and reinforcing concepts in other curriculum areas, including social studies, mathematics, and science.

▼   ▼   ▼

From the beginning of the picture word inductive model to the end, the teacher models seeking, thinking, and using learning while providing instruction that engages students in seeking, thinking, and using their accumulating knowledge. I love using the PWIM because we can take students—individually and as groups—as far as they can conceptually "see" in language learning. There are no artificial caps on what can be learned.

6

Working with Older Beginning Readers

This chapter is for teachers working with older students who are beginning readers, or for teachers working with students who have not mastered many of the basic literacy skills needed for success in school, especially students in 4th–8th grades. To help you understand my teaching stance or philosophy, especially as it relates to these older students, I share my views on the nature of the literacy challenge faced when working with these students and suggest ways you can tailor the PWIM for these older beginning readers. I reinforce the ideas that investing in teaching and the PWIM can play a role in consolidating curricular and instructional principles in developing literacy for everyone.

Some things do not change, despite students' ages and abilities. The constant instructional goals remain critical in lesson and unit design and in teacher-and-student interactions: (1) building sight vocabulary; (2) helping students build confidence in their ability to learn; and (3) teaching students how to inquire into language and use what they know and find to read and write and participate fully in their own educational progress. The use of an integrated language arts approach and the language arts curriculum goals as described briefly in Chapter 4 remain the same; however, different aspects of language skills and processes receive more or less emphasis depending on the abilities of the students.

We have many students in U.S. schools in 4th grade and above who need work on the same reading and writing processes and skills addressed in chapters 1–5. These students are in peril in our school system and in our society because of their literacy levels. As we create instructional environments for these students, a few of the teaching tools we can bring to the task include integrated modes of teaching and learning, interrelated curriculum work, continuous rapid diagnosis, and a knowledge of how to use what they already know. The PWIM is one of several teaching strategies that allow us to pack our toolkit efficiently.

Modifying the PWIM

Major reasons for modifying the PWIM for older students are differences in what they bring to the PWIM as language learners and differences in age and maturity. Modifications necessary for older beginning readers include grouping patterns, use of and types of pictures, and pace through the moves of the model.

The difference in age means some of the hokey, fun things we can do as we teach 5-year-old students we cannot do as we teach those who are 10 to 14 years old. For instance, it just doesn't work to call older students word detectives, language sleuths, or investigators; or to use the sheer force of your personality to induce a whole classroom of 13-year-old students into analyzing a word. However, your joy in language exploration, lessons that place students in the role of inquiring into how language works, lesson design that requires participation in productive and engaging work, and never giving up on bringing them into fuller literacy are professional gifts that we can give these older beginning readers.

We must avoid thinking of older beginning readers as less capable learners. Although a 12-year-old may have a smaller number of synapses connecting neurons in the brain than a 6-year-old, many people continue to acquire vocabulary and increase their skill and sophistication in language use throughout their lives. We do not know the effect of synaptic proliferation (a dramatic increase in the number of synapses that connect the neurons in the brain occurring from birth or infancy to around age 10) or synaptic elimination (a decrease in the overall number of synaptic connections) on human learners. We do have data from research in cognitive psychology, developmental psychology, and social and behavioral psychology about the effects of an enriched environment on human learning; much is available from these areas of study that we can use in designing instruction. There is even some evidence from neuroscience about "experience-dependent brain plasticity"; in simple terms, the idea is that the brain continues to create new synapses in response to new experiences throughout the animal's life. (See Bruer, 1997, pp. 4–16, for an excellent discussion of the brain and education.)

I take the optimistic view (even more so as I age!): With rich and appropriate instructional environments, almost everyone who is not severely neurologically impaired can continue to learn and develop. Part of the literacy challenge with these older beginning readers resides in finding better combinations of instructional strategies, allowing enough time for learning to occur, and helping them learn to attend to instruction when other realms of their lives may have little or no support for academic learning.

Grouping Patterns

You may still engage in whole-class instruction, particularly if you have a heterogeneous group or a combination class in grades 4–6. If you have a small self-contained class, or if you tutor students one at a time, the PWIM still works for you and your students. In a tutorial situation, though little is done with building the learning community and less with the social aspects of communication, the teacher and student can take turns selecting pictures.

Pace

How much faster the lessons move from identifying items in the picture, to classifying these words, to writing paragraphs simply depends on the abilities of the students. The time between generating words and generating sentences and paragraphs by students generally shortens with older students, but not always.

As in kindergarten through much of 2nd grade, the emphasis on spelling and vocabulary development continues, but the phonetic, structural, and contextual analysis becomes more limited and more focused, for example:

• On patterns of need, diagnosed from what students say or write;

• On exceptions to general rules (if the plural of *house* is *houses* and *blouse* is *blouses*, why isn't the plural of *mouse*, *mouses*? What about the plural for *rice*?); and

• On language conventions that must be memorized, such as the difference in meaning and spelling between the *capital* city and the *capitol* building.

Shaping Instruction

With older beginning readers, the teacher or class can designate certain words for the word list or word bank, while continuing to have all relevant terms and descriptions on the chart and all the sentences on printouts.

While these students may not have mastered useful phonics generalizations and spelling patterns, they usually have many of the mechanical skills emphasized at the early primary grades. For example, older beginning readers probably do not need to review the formation of letters, the names of letters, the difference between a letter and a word, the difference between a word and a sentence, and spacing between words.

Many older beginning readers have general understandings about the English language system that they are unaware of and are not using as readers and writers. These students' cognitions about how the English language works may range from simple to complex. For example, older students often recognize utilitarian spelling patterns (e.g., *q* is almost always followed by *u*) and useful phonics generalizations (e.g., when a word begins with /kn/ the *k* is silent or when a word ends in /ck/ as in *check* the last phoneme is /k/, and words do not begin with /ck/). Older students have understandings about sentence and paragraph content that can be built upon, such as the recognition of information that belongs together around a central idea in either English or Spanish. For students whose native language is Spanish, the similarities in the alphabet and in many of the phonemes (/b/, /d/, /f/) and syntax (as in the subject and predicate order in sentences or the functions of modifiers) can be used.

As you know, time is precious. Rapid diagnosis and the use of its results during and between lessons allow us to continuously shape instruction. So we engage in constant on-our-feet diagnosis; help students access and use what they already know; and teach and model the similarities of the cognitive processes of reading and writing. While our daily objectives focus on helping students become increasingly literate, our long-term goals include helping them learn more efficiently in school and helping them develop lifelong learning skills. After one or two picture word cycles, you'll know what most individuals can do and how they perceive themselves as language learners; you'll also know about their general academic self-esteem.

Sequence of the Picture Word Inductive Model

Using the 10 moves of the PWIM (see Chapter 2, Figure 2.1), I've listed common modifications and extensions that may help you use the PWIM with older beginning readers. Adapt the PWIM to your situation and students, perhaps taking some of these suggestions and blending them with your own ideas. My list of modifications is aimed for students in 3rd grade or higher who need to increase their literacy skills.

1. Ideas about pictures

- Choose additional pictures.
- Select pictures and photographs that support social studies and science units being taught. For social studies, use pictures of the neighborhood, the community, the town, or events to simultaneously anchor and expand students' explorations of the characteristics of these settings. For science, choose pictures of different animals and mammals in various settings (urban, rural, and rainforest), or plants (in houses, deserts, and oceans), or a variety of businesses and services (a dairy, the lunchroom workers, a dental hygienist). The list of possibilities is as extensive as the concepts and topics within the curriculum.

The picture and the process of converting it into a picture word chart continues to promote the expansion of students' vocabulary, the mechanics of spelling and language usage, and the use of observation in providing content and evidence in oral and written discourse. While there is continuing emphasis on phonetic and structural analysis, there is emphasis on content and what the picture shows. Particularly after 3rd grade, the picture can open an area of study and serve as a focal point for discussions, examples, and the exploration of a subject.

- Students can take their own photographs of scenes around their community, their neighborhood, the places they visit on field trips or beyond the school; develop their own picture word charts; classify their words; and write their own informative paragraphs or stories. However, individual exercises should not replace the use of the PWIM with the whole class.

2. Identifying items and ideas in the picture

- Make the first lesson a group discussion about the picture if you have students who are shy or who have extreme language deficits.
- Spend more time discussing items in the pictures than you would with younger students. For example, you might bring in and have available during recess several different sports balls and have students talk

about the games, and how the balls are alike and different. Activities like these build on what students know and expand their reading and spelling of these words.

• Students can scan, read, and gather additional information to identify items in the picture. For example, if you presented a picture of a farm with animals and equipment, you might provide a selection of fiction and nonfiction books about farm animals and life on the farm, which would expose students to additional resources and allow them to discover additional words or items to add to the picture word chart.

3. Labeling the picture parts
• Label items in the students' native language.
• Label items in two languages if that will be useful for your students.
• Use the sequence of seeing, saying, and spelling each word as an option, not a requirement.

4. Reading and reviewing the picture word chart
• Begin the PWIM by reading and reviewing the chart together daily, but move the class toward silent practice and individual reading.
• Select certain words for reading or spelling emphasis.

5. Reading and classifying the words
• Students need to become increasingly articulate about the categories they form and their attributes. For example, *cheese, peach, chilled juice, inchworm*—all have /ch/; together they make only one sound; and that sound is /ch/ as in *church.* Or, *red car, big chrome bumper, tan leather seats, small steering wheel, four chrome wheels, wide tires*—all describe the car in the picture.
• Students who are having difficulty pronouncing the words can use the *American Heritage Talking Dictionary on CD-ROM.* They can use their word cards for the correct spelling of the words.

6. Reading and reviewing the word chart

- Same as Step 4.

7. Adding words

- Ask students to find many words that belong to useful categories. Some of these words can be generated as part of the lesson; however, place greater responsibility on older students for accumulating additional words for homework and classwork than you would on younger students.

8. Creating titles

- To introduce your students to the idea of creating titles, read to them the titles and first paragraphs or pages from well-written, informative books. Providing good examples of titles and explaining the relationship between titles and paragraphs advertises books you want students to read, emphasizes concepts being taught in other curriculum areas, and allows beginning readers to hear a fluent reader engaging with prose.

- Take opportunities to pursue, through paragraph development, the several equally accurate titles your students may suggest (suggestions from individuals and from groups). Work on denotations and cultural implications as they surface.

9. Generating sentences and paragraphs

- Turn categories formed in #5 into paragraphs so students can understand how classifying content can help them organize their ideas into informative prose.

- Classify sentences into groups that form the basis for paragraph development.

- Gather additional information from nonfiction books; as information increases, so will the length of group compositions and individual compositions developed around different aspects of the picture. One well-organized paragraph, however, may still be a worthy goal for group and individual work.

10. Reading and reviewing sentences and paragraphs

• Provide regular opportunities for students to do independent writing in their journals and create new sentences related to the chart.

• Ask students to serve as audience and supporting collaborators to help each other develop ideas.

• Provide opportunities to put together multiple-paragraph pieces related to social studies content and to develop study guides.

Whatever teaching strategy is being used, we desperately need these students to engage in the effort to move forward into literacy: thus, the structure of lessons should minimize the possibility of passive participation and maximize student participation in their progress.

The Literacy Challenge with Older Students

The struggle with how to teach students to read well is always with us. How do we make our attempts—to help all children learn to read well enough to handle the materials they encounter in school and the materials they encounter as productive citizens—more productive?

Early in the schooling experience of most children, educators can identify the children for whom the system is not working. We generally know by the end of 1st grade which students are not learning to read or which students are not responding to the instruction the system is providing (Juel, 1988, 1992). We also know that the correlation of their reading performance with the probability they will drop out of school is significant at the .001 level (Garnier, Stein, & Jacobs, 1997); we are certain by the end of 3rd grade (Lloyd, 1978; Juel, 1988); we see the cumulative results of this lack of literacy at the beginning of middle school; and we see the tremendous number of students who quit school in 9th and 10th grades.

Large urban districts are especially concerned about two well-documented national trends: (1) U.S. schools have been least successful in teaching children from low-income families to read (Cooley, 1993; McGill-Franzen, 1994); (2) Of the black youth who remain in school through 12th grade, 46 percent cannot read at a basic level; and 39 percent of Hispanic youth who remain in school through 12th grade cannot read at a basic level (Mullis, Campbell, & Farstrup, 1993). Moving back to the middle school level, the National Education Longitudinal Study of 8th graders (Hafner, Ingles, Schneider, & Stevenson, 1990; Kaufman, McMillen, & Bradby, 1992) reports that 6.8 percent of its 8th grade cohort had dropped out of school within the first two years of the study. Hispanic students and black students dropped out of the cohort at a rate twice that of their peers.

We have spent millions of hours and millions of dollars to help students of all ages who read and write poorly or not at all. And our success rate is not good. One hypothesis for explaining this poor return on our literacy investment questions the curriculum content and instructional strategies used in many of the compensatory and remedial programs. Serious concerns about remedial programs have been raised:

• Instruction in many remedial and compensatory programs has been influenced by "the legacy of 'slow it down and make it more concrete'" (Allington, 1991). So little of the language curriculum is presented, and without the higher-order concepts, that many students cannot pull the skills pieces together and progress as readers.

• Oversimplification of content such that the instruction being used actually impedes literacy learning (Roehler, 1991).

• The time available for students in remedial programs to engage in reading is often less than that for their peers because the emphasis is on skills-based instruction instead of on reading and on learning reading strategies (Johnston & Allington, 1991).

• Instruction for good and poor readers frequently varies: Poor readers often experience lessons with less emphasis on the final performance (reading), and more emphasis on drills and materials that focus on fragments of literacy performance, as well as reinforcement of old reading strategies. Good readers are taught more effective reading strategies (Allington, 1983; Applebee, Langer, & Mullis, 1988).

• The less responsive students are to the curriculum and instruction they are experiencing, the more likely the educational system is to fragment their curriculum and daily lesson content—focusing instruction on the lowest-level subskills and losing sight of the student performance goals of reading and writing as communication (Pearson, 1992, p. 1080).

• Remedial programs usually take a synthesis of skills approach, teaching phonetic and structural analysis, comprehension skills, and vocabulary piece by piece, with the idea that the students will be able to put the pieces together at some time and read and write. The better students are given more opportunities to put all the pieces together as they read material at their level and more opportunities to build the concepts necessary for word recognition and comprehension.

• Instruction in writing is subject to the same criticism. The program for the more proficient students tends to be balanced among writing, communicating the message, and using standard grammatical conventions. Middle school and secondary students who have difficulty communicating through writing, however, receive instructional feedback that appears to emphasize grammar and mechanics, not the message each student is trying to communicate (Applebee, Langer, Jenkins, Mullis, & Foertsch, 1990; Gentile, 1992). Low performing students also have less time to write than high-performing students (Applebee, Langer, Mullis, Latham, & Gentile, 1994).

Researchers who have analyzed the operations and results of the compensatory and remedial reading programs offer much for us to think about as we work with these students or with teachers responsible

for instructing them. For example, when students are placed in remedial programs, does the amount of reading and writing they do become
reduced in favor of an unbalanced emphasis on skills taught in isolation
from the acts of reading and writing? Are these skills taught piecemeal,
disconnected from personal inquiry into how language works?

Allington (1994) and Moore and Davenport (1988) address how
efficient schools have become in sorting those who can perform in the
current curriculum and instructional program from those who cannot
perform satisfactorily. Allington strongly recommends that schools
spend less time and money on sorting students into special programs
and groups and spend more time on providing instructional interventions and environments that teach all students.

Changing the Literacy Achievement Picture

When I work with schools in schoolwide action research or improving
language literacy, I find belief in what I call the M & Ms of school
improvement: materials, movement, and money. In other words, the
people I work with think that if they just had more of those three
things, they would have the magic wands for improving student
achievement. In facilitating and working as critical friend with these
faculties, I often ask them to check their school improvement or district improvement plans. Is the solution to low student achievement or
to helping remedial readers too heavily weighted toward materials
(investing heavily in new commercial programs? the right language
kit? the right computer and software package?); toward movement
(moving students into other classrooms, adding Title I classes, adding
special education classes, forming alternative schools?); or toward
money (seeking or expending funds on additional programs? adding
staff?)?

I've spent many days, weeks, and months in remedial reading and
compensatory classes during the last 25 years, and one of the major
similarities across time and place has been an incredible reliance on

commercial programs and skills development materials to improve reading achievement. I've seen many caring teachers who were primarily skillful materials and records managers. Yet, if these students were independent learners, if they could learn through materials, they would not be in these classes or groups.

Our remedial and compensatory programs may have continued as they are because of the belief that all we have to do is decrease class size and student achievement will improve. The stress of working with students from different backgrounds, the increased public attention to student achievement, and politics keep this belief fresh. This belief operates across U.S. districts and many states despite more than 30 years of reduced class sizes and small-group work for these students with an abysmal success rate in reading achievement. (In many districts, successful redesignation from remedial programs back into regular classroom programs is from 4 percent to 10 percent.) Of course, I like smaller classes. I was generally less fatigued with classes of 20 students than with classes of 30 to 35 students. I think it would take a reduction to 4 students per teacher, however, to make class size alone a durable factor in improved student achievement.

To improve student achievement in reading, the best investment is probably in ourselves—expanding the number of teaching strategies we have ready for use and expanding our understanding of the structure of the discipline of language arts. This is something that we—public school educators—have some direct control over. We cannot quickly change neighborhoods or home environments or socioeconomic circumstances, but we can change the range of instructional opportunities and the learning environments available for students and for ourselves.

We have the capacity to provide powerful literacy instruction. Although it would undoubtedly require extended staff development at the school or district level, we could provide our older students who are still learning to read with much more teacher and student interaction in which highly literate persons guide and facilitate their development in reading and writing and communicating. These students need teachers who will take them into a world that is currently inaccessible, and in some ways invisible, to them.

Teaching Works

We are teachers and we have chosen our profession because we believe teaching works. Using a strategy such as the PWIM—or any of the inquiry-oriented and explicit instruction strategies—does not take much in the way of materials or movement. What it does require is continuous, focused teacher and student interaction and continuous action-research-on-your-feet instruction and a good basic knowledge of how the English language works. To that end, are school and district improvement plans weighted heavily toward expanding the staff's teaching repertoire and instructional range? Improving the staff's skills takes time, money, and focus—but it is probably the best investment a school or district can make for improving student achievement.

Applying and Consolidating Curricular and Instructional Principles

The picture word inductive model is not magic, nor do I mean to imply that it is a panacea for all literacy woes. It is just one powerful teaching strategy from a range of many available, both documented and undocumented. However, part of my professional affection for the PWIM is that it allows me to apply several curricular and instructional principles I believe in as a language arts teacher and educator. The PWIM allows me to consolidate my beliefs about what works in developing literacy:

• A multidimensional approach: Teaching several aspects of literacy simultaneously and using multiple teaching/learning strategies

• An inquiry-orientation: Teaching students how to learn and how to construct knowledge

• A collaborative orientation: Teaching students to learn together and support each others' efforts

- A formative assessment orientation: Using what students can do, what they notice, and the language arts objectives and skills of the curriculum to shape the next move in the lesson, the next lesson, or the next unit
- Explicit instruction: Using modeling, demonstrations, explanations, and applications to build knowledge and skill
- Metacognitive control: Developing students' knowledge and use of their own cognitive resources.

My beliefs come from my own experience as a teacher and from studying our professional knowledge base, gathering ideas, and trying them out. I could give you personal experiences and stories, research studies and syntheses, and reports of scholarly commentary until your eyes glaze. Instead, I ask you to think about your own set of operational beliefs that shape your teaching stance, interaction with students, and lesson design. Do you see ways that the PWIM could help you consolidate valued instructional principles? Do you see aspects of curriculum that it could enhance?

One of the advantages of the picture word inductive model is its respect for the learner. Respect is a valuable asset when working with students who have difficulty learning to read. Students generate the words and the sentences that will be learned and classified; they gather additional words and information from trade books and other resources. They learn from each other and from the teacher. The concepts they own about how language works are used to support instruction and are constantly being extended—whatever their native language. Whether the student is 6 years old, 12 years old, or 36 years old, whatever is available as a language foundation can, through teacher and student interaction and collective effort, be a base for rapid literacy development.

A positive aspect in addressing the literacy challenge is that these older students, whatever their native language or home environment, bring more knowledge with them than 6-year-olds. The older students are more mature; if they choose to engage, they can make rapid progress, moving ahead in reading and literacy much faster than the average 6-year-old. Many older students who have not learned to read and write well are resourceful persons in their daily lives inside and outside of school; one of our aims in a rapid literacy development program is to have them use their natural cognitive resources for academic purposes.

Endnote

My belief in the power of reading well and widely led me into teaching and into the English language arts. Twenty-seven years later I still believe that reading can open windows on the world and provide possibilities in life far different and far better than what you might experience daily. Reading allows interaction with persons and cultures like and unlike your own family and surroundings; reading is an avenue for becoming highly educated and is available to almost everyone. Reading can help you see choices you did not see before—choices that can make you who you are.

We—as teachers—hold the keys to literacy for many students, the keys that provide access and choice. For students, the more words they have in their listening and speaking vocabularies, the more understanding they have of the world around them; the more words they have in their reading and writing vocabularies, the more control and choice they have both in and out of school, along with greater access to knowledge and experience and greater potential for teaching themselves; the more understanding they have of how language works, the more powerful they can be as communicators and citizens.

One of the challenges facing teachers is to tap into the natural ability of young people to seek meaning and enjoy social interchange. We inquire into our surroundings from the moment of birth. Very early we desire to be part of and in control of some aspects of our environment.

We want to belong in our cultural surroundings; language facility helps to provide cultural security and, in many cases, academic success. By teaching students to read and write in ways that closely resemble how young children acquire the speaking vocabulary of their culture, we can perhaps help students progress more quickly and effectively. I am not saying reading and writing are natural biological processes, but I am saying we can design instruction so that students can learn by analyzing how language works and by actively, cognitively engaging them in this analysis.

Our journey into teaching and language literacy never ends.

▼   ▼   ▼

I have written this book as a hymn for language learning and teaching. It is my accolade to what is and to what is possible. Through form, tone, and voice, I have tried to take readers into classrooms of skillful teachers using a simple but powerful teaching strategy that brings many students rapidly and naturally into greater literacy. I hope I have tempted you into trying the picture word inductive model in your classroom or school and watching what happens for students. My success depends on what you do now.

Appendix 1:
Explicit Instruction and Suggestions

When planning units using the picture word inductive model, teachers move the lessons between inductive activity and explicit instruction. You may opt to provide explicit instruction on any aspect of the language system, including those that you want to introduce or reinforce. Explicit instruction may involve developing skills in phonics or structural analysis, explaining and modeling reading comprehension processes, and explaining and modeling any aspect of writing craft.

Explicit instruction is a training model for skill development. By that, I mean that explicit instruction entails designing instruction and follow-up activities that provide information about the skill and its use; demonstrate the skill; and offer practice, application and transfer of the skill. Through this process of explicit instruction, which includes teacher explanations, teacher modeling, student practices, and many student applications of the concept or skills, we train students to recognize and use language concepts, generalizations, skills, and processes. For example, to provide explicit instruction in skill development in phonics or structural or contextual analysis, design lessons and activities with these components:

- Clear explanation of the immediate purpose of the word recognition skill (e.g., to determine pronunciation or meaning of a word),
- Clear explanation of the ultimate purpose (e.g., understanding text),
- Modeling of word recognition skills (e.g., thinking aloud about how students use the skill and when),
- Examples of instances in which the skill could be needed,
- Guided student practice with the skill being taught, and

• Immediate application of the skill in reading and writing activities.

These lessons can be used for work on phonetic analysis and phonemic awareness (understanding that spoken words comprise speech sounds that may be represented by one, two, three, or more letters). Explicit lessons are particularly useful for teaching structural analysis and contextual analysis. For lesson examples, see Graves, Watts, and Graves, 1994; Nagy, Winsor, Osborn, and O'Flahavan, 1994; and Copeland, Winsor, and Osborn, 1994, for suggestions on phonemic awareness.

If appropriate, phonics lessons can move from simple onsets and rimes into more complex use of these patterns in multisyllabic words. Phonics lessons such as these help students to build skills in decoding words by analogy to one known word, by analogy to several known words sharing a spelling pattern, and by applying generalized spelling patterns (Cunningham, 1975/1976; Gaskins, Downer, Anderson, Cunningham, Gaskins, & Schommer, 1988).

A reminder about explicit instruction in structural analysis: Research studies and syntheses, though few in number, indicate that instruction in structural analysis is especially valuable for low-achieving students (Graves, 1986; White, Power, & White, 1989; Nagy et al., 1994).

For extended explanations of using explicit instruction in teaching reading comprehension, see Pearson and Dole, 1987; and Dole, Duffy, Roehler, and Pearson, 1991.

Additional examples of inductive lessons can be found in Joyce and Calhoun (1998). And explanations of explicit instruction in teaching composition are available in Englert, Raphael, Anderson, Anthony, and Stevens, 1991.

Appendix 2:
Concept Attainment

What can we do in the PWIM lessons when we want to ensure student recognition and clarification of a concept? One possibility is to use a structured inquiry called concept attainment, which is designed to clarify ideas and to introduce aspects of content.

Concept attainment is the search for and identification of attributes that can be used to distinguish examples of a given group or category from nonexamples (Bruner, Goodnow, & Austin, 1967, p. 233). In concept attainment, students figure out the attributes of a group or category that has already been formed by the teacher or another student—as in Chapter 3 (p. 46), when Ms. Lewis had students study categories of words that she compiled from the word list.

As students conduct their inquiries within the framework of the picture word inductive model, you will find that their categories are not always precise or exactly as you would like them to be. For example, students may put words beginning with *cl* and *cr* together (when you want them to look beyond the initial consonant) and gloss over the differences, possibly having difficulty recategorizing words into groups other than those that begin with *cl* and *cr*. Also, students may not discover important categories in the picture word list or they may develop a group of words in which they have seen only some of the attributes, such as the multiple attribute category of double medial consonants in closed-syllable words (e.g., rabbit, ladder). Part of the concept attainment model requires that students compare and contrast examples that contain the attributes of the concept with examples that do not contain those attributes until they have 100 percent mastery.

Here's a brief scenario of concept attainment being used to clarify a beginning phonics and spelling concept for students who are learning English as a second language.

▼   ▼   ▼

Ora Kwo is teaching a lesson on English to her students in Hong Kong. She has a chart in the front of the room with two columns labeled Yes and No. She puts *clean* under Yes and *help* under No.

"Take a look at these two words. How are they alike and how are they different? *Clean* has the attributes of our category. *Help* does not." She places cards containing two more words on the chart: *clear* and *trim*. Then Ms. Kwo says, "Now examine this pair. *Clear* has the attributes we are looking for. *Help* does not. What do *clear* and *clean* have in common that *help* and *trim* do not?"

She presents *clip* and *hip* and asks the students to compare and contrast them and to try to discover what the positive examples have in common that they do not share with the negative examples. Ms. Kwo adds *clap* and *lap* to the list and asks the class if they had to change their reasons for categorizing their words. A few students raise their hands to say yes. At this point, Ms. Kwo presents several other pairs of words: *cling, ring; climb, limb; club, tree*. Then she presents *lip* and asks the students whether they believe, on the basis of their current idea of the concept, if it belongs to the yes category. Of the students, 26 of the 30 students correctly identify the word as a negative example. She infers that the 26 are concentrating on the *cl* while the others are still not sure whether having either a *c* or an *l* qualifies the word. Therefore, she presents these words to be classified: *clue, flue; clarify, rarify; clack, lack*.

After a few minutes, she adds *crack* to the board. All of the students identify the word as not belonging to the group. Next Ms. Kwo presents *clank*, which the class identifies as a yes. She asks them to share their current hypotheses: The positives begin with *cl* and sound like the beginning of *clap*. She has them identify what is not critical: meanings of the words, endings, and the number of letters. Ms. Kwo asks the class to turn the words they rejected into words to accept for the list (e.g., transforming *an* to *clan*, until she is satisfied that the concept is clear). The teacher asks the class to find additional examples of the category for homework.

▼   ▼   ▼

We have looked in on a concept attainment lesson in phonics and spelling. In this case, the concept being clarified by students was the initial consonant cluster /cl/. The concept attainment process helps to ensure that students learn the attributes that define a concept (the defining attributes) and can distinguish those from other attributes that are important but do not define the concept. All words, for example, contain letters, but the presence of letters does not define the concept of "words that begin with the initial consonant cluster /cl/." As we teach students with this method, we help them become more efficient in attaining useful concepts. Concept attainment is a great addition to PWIM units and is an excellent direct instruction model for language study with beginning readers and second language learners, particularly for mastery of phonics generalizations and structural analysis concepts.

This explanation was derived from Bruce Joyce, Marsha Weil, and Beverly Showers, *Models of Teaching*, 5th ed., 1996, pp. 161–178. See this source for addition information on using the concept attainment model.

Appendix 3:
Vocabulary Development

It's easy to use the picture word inductive model for vocabulary development because it emphasizes building a large sight vocabulary and using inductive and explicit instruction to teach the application of phonetic and structural generalizations. Of course, every teacher has language arts components that are major emphases and we can generally cite various sources of support. Vocabulary development is one of my emphases across all grade levels and subject areas, and here are some of the reasons and sources of support.

Words are used to communicate ideas. The more words you own, the better you can communicate; the better you are at acquiring words, the more control you have over your own educational progress. Thus, ideas that shape the teaching and learning strategy for vocabulary development address building vocabulary size and acquiring and increasing efficient use of word recognition skills.

In terms of general academic success, vocabulary knowledge is one of the best predictors of overall verbal intelligence, yielding correlations of .80 (Anderson & Freebody, 1981; Sternberg & Powell, 1983). Each word a student can comprehend and use appropriately adds to personal cognitive processing abilities. Plus, "one of the most consistent findings of educational research is that having a small vocabulary portends poor school performance" (Anderson & Nagy, 1992, p. 14).

Expanding Vocabulary. Language arts scholars agree that vocabulary building is important in developing literacy no matter what the age of students; there is some agreement in the knowledge base about the efficiency of vocabulary development through reading—simply get students reading and they will build their vocabularies. Sternberg's (1987) essay presents a persuasive argument that "most vocabulary is learned from context." And, Nagy, Herman, and Anderson (1985) argue that accumulating vocabulary through reading is about 10 times more efficient than the common methods of vocabulary instruction.

What best accompanies extensive reading (and a language-rich environment) in expanding vocabulary is surrounded by debate. Some sources indicate that direct instruction in vocabulary is so inefficient as to be useless (Krashen, 1993), that vocabulary instruction is rare (Durkin, 1978–79), that the instruction incorporated in the textbooks recommends weak teaching procedures (Jenkins, Stein, & Wysocki, 1984; Durkin, 1986), and that the most common classroom vocabulary program uses approaches that do not work well, such as word lists from which students study the definitions, compose sentences, and are tested (Anderson & Nagy, 1992). On top of this, for the last 12 to 15 years, there have been two competing lines of inquiry about what works in building vocabulary: reading widely versus systematic instruction (Graves, 1992).

Results from the research on systematic instruction indicate that the more effective methods of vocabulary instruction use both definitional and contextual information, involve students in deeper processing (thinking of similar material, of similar classes of words, analogies, associations), and provide multiple exposures to the words (Stahl & Fairbanks, 1986; Stahl, 1999). These approaches include the mnemonic keyword method (Levin, McCormick, Miller, Berry, & Pressley, 1982; Pressley, Levin, & McDaniel, 1987) and classification accompanied by defining and sentence production tasks. The more effective approaches to expanding vocabulary through instruction require more active involvement by the teacher in planning and delivering instruction and more cognitive engagement by the students than commonly found.

Skill and speed in phonetic, structural, and contextual analysis help us to identify and confirm words. These skills and language principles can be learned through combinations of analyses, where sight vocabulary words are classified until the phonetic and structural principles are developed (the approach dominant in the inductive phases of PWIM), or synthetically, where letters and combinations of letters are studied in relation to the sounds and meanings that are attached to them (Ehri, 1994; Graves, 1992; Nagy et al., 1994).

Along with expanding vocabulary size, another reason for teaching a base of sight words is that until a student has a sight word vocabulary of at least 50 words there is "no meaningful context within which phonics instruction could take place" (Graves, Watts, & Graves, 1994, p. 92).

What about high-frequency words? Should students engage in rapid mastery of the 10 words (*the, of, and, a, to, in, is, you, that, it*) that make up 20 percent of the words they will see in continuous print, or the 200 high-frequency sight words that make up about 60 percent of text they are likely to read (Gunning, 1996), or the 50 highest frequency words (Peregoy & Boyle, 1997, from Mason & Au, 1990)? Teaching a list of sight words is not a popular idea in the current mood of engaging students in authentic tasks. Imagine how difficult it would be to read even the simplest materials if we did not own the 10 high-frequency words as automatic sight words? Imagine trying to analyze or decode them through a synthetic phonics approach.

Preferably in 1st grade, but at least by the end of 2nd grade, we want students to achieve automaticity in reading the 200 most common words in English text because they occur so often. Many of these words are irregularly spelled or phonetically irregular (*one, of, are, were, where, there*); instant recognition of these words allows the brain to focus on comprehending more content-laden words (e.g., *smoke, house, jeans*) and on executing higher-level comprehension processes.

Developing Word Identification Skills. Skilled reading depends not just on knowing a large number of words, but on being able to deal effectively with new words. What happens when one cannot read a word automatically?

Skilled readers have at least three sources of information or three word identification strategies to use when dealing with new words: phonics to determine the word's pronunciation, structural analysis to determine and confirm a word's meaning and its pronunciation, and context to infer and confirm the word's meaning (Nagy et al., 1994). Skilled readers see all the letters in words, focus on patterns (groups of letters they are used to seeing together in terms of either word order or word meaning), then use context to confirm their recognition of the word or to redirect their efforts if the word spoken internally does not fit the meaning of the text.

The PWIM units can support instruction in all three aspects of word identification skills: phonetic analysis, structural analysis, and contextual analysis. The units can include formal and informal assessment of current skills; inductive lessons in phonetic analysis, structural analysis, and contextual analysis in areas of identified need; explicit instruction in these same forms of analysis; and extensive reading and writing for practice and consolidation of the skills (both new and current skills).

For all students, but especially for students whose first language is not English and for students with limited speaking vocabularies, the *American Heritage Dictionary on CD-ROM* is very useful: words are pronounced, used in context, and defined. If you have several students who speak English poorly or not at all, a talking dictionary and a translator program would be ideal—for students and teacher.

To acquire fluency in reading, students need to acquire a large sight vocabulary, to learn to use the most common phonetic and structural principles, and to use context to help them determine word meaning. The PWIM helps us help students build these reading competencies.

Appendix 4:
Reading Aloud

Reading aloud to the students is one way to encourage reading, model fluent reading, and share reader responses. Children who are read to at home read more on their own; students whose teachers read to them read more; even college students who are read to read more (Morrow & Weinstein, 1986; Neuman, 1986; and Pitts, 1986). In Stahl's (1999) research synthesis on vocabulary development, he makes three suggestions about what to do to improve vocabulary knowledge: (1) increase the amount of reading that children do, (2) teach word meanings, and (3) "read to children—even older children who are not traditionally read to" (p. 13).

While there is general agreement on the importance of reading aloud to children in and out of school, a survey of reading- aloud practices in 537 elementary classrooms indicated that one-third of the teachers surveyed rarely read aloud to students, and for those teachers who were reading aloud regularly, few read nonfiction (Hoffman, Roser, & Battle, 1993). My colleagues and I estimate that for most students, their opportunity to hear something read well on a daily basis decreases each year they are in school.

Students should hear something read well every day. By reading aloud to students, teachers invite them to enter the world of reading. Reading aloud offers students experience with the rhythms of the English language, a model of enjoyment and learning from print, and an opportunity to be engaged with text. Reading aloud is especially beneficial for low achievers (Bridge 1989; Winograd & Bridge, 1995) and works to increase students' comprehension and vocabulary test scores (Cochran-Smith, 1988). Through their choices of material to read aloud, teachers essentially recommend books or selections to students, frequently inspiring students to read more (Greaney & Hegarty, 1987; Wendelin & Zinck, 1983).

Here are my tips for reading aloud as you use the picture word inductive model:

- Select primarily nonfiction material.
- Choose passages that capture powerful or useful concepts.
- Practice reading the selection aloud before you share with students.
- Plan a few comments to encourage class discussion, such as what drew you to that passage, how you figured out the message, or how you will use the information.
- Use the passage to emphasize varied concepts in the curriculum.
- Budget your time—segments of reading aloud can productively range from 5 to 20 minutes when discussion is included.

For additional ideas on reading aloud see Moss, 1995.

Bibliography

Adams, M. J. (1990). *Beginning to read: Thinking and learning about print*. Cambridge, MA: MIT Press.

Adams, A. H., Johnson, M. S., & Connors, J. M. (1980). *Success in kindergarten reading and writing*. Glenview, IL: Good Year Books.

Allington, R. L. (1983). The reading instruction provided readers of differing reading ability. *Elementary School Journal, 83,* 548–559.

Allington, R. L. (1991). The legacy of "slow it down and make it more concrete." In J. Zutell & S. McCormick (Eds.), *Learner factors/teacher factors: Issues in literacy research and instruction* (pp. 19–30). Chicago: National Reading Conference.

Allington, R. L. (1994). What's special about special programs for children who find learning to read difficult? *Journal of Reading Behaviour, 26*(1), 95–115.

Anderson, R. C., & Freebody, P. (1981). Vocabulary knowledge. In J.Guthrie (Ed.), *Comprehension and teaching: Research reviews* (pp. 77–117). Newark, DE: International Reading Association.

Anderson, R. C., & Nagy, W. E. (1992, Winter). The vocabulary conundrum. *American Educator, 16*(4), 14–18, 45–47. (ERIC Document Reproduction Service No. ED 354 489)

Applebee, A. N., Langer, J. A., Jenkins, L., Mullis, I. V. S., & Foertsch, M. (1990). *Learning to write in our nation's schools: Instruction and achievement in 1988 at grades 4, 8, and 12*. Princeton, NJ: Educational Testing Service; National Assessment of Educational Progress. (ED 318 038)

Applebee, A. N., Langer, J. A., & Mullis, I. V. S. (1988). *Who reads best? Factors related to reading achievement in grades 3, 7, and 11*. Princeton, NJ: National Assessment of Educational Progress.

Applebee, A. N., Langer, J. A., Mullis, I. V. S., Latham, A. S., & Gentile, C. A. (1994). *NAEP 1992 writing report card*. Princeton, NJ: National Assessment of Educational Progress.

Bloome, D. (Ed.). (1987). *Literacy and schooling*. Norwood, NJ: Ablex.

Bridge, C. (1989). Beyond the basal in beginning reading. In P. Winograd, K. Wixson, & M. Lipson (Eds.), *Improving basal reading instruction* (pp. 177–209). New York: Teachers College Press.

Bruer, J. T. (1997). Education and the brain: A bridge too far. *Educational Researcher, 26*(8) 4–16.

Bruner, J., Goodnow J. J., & Austin, G. A. (1967). *A study of thinking*. New York: Science Editions.

Chall, J. S. (1967). *Learning to read: The great debate*. New York: McGraw-Hill.

Clark, H. H., & Clark, E. V. (1977). *Psychology and language: An introduction to psycholinguistics*. New York: Harcourt, Brace, Jovanovich.

Clymer, T. (1996/1963). The utility of phonic generalizations in the primary grades. *The Reading Teacher, 50*(3), pp.182–187.

Cochran-Smith, M. (1988). Mediating: An important role for the reading teacher. In C. Hedley & J. Hicks (Eds.), *Reading and the special learner* (pp. 109–139). Norwood, NJ: Ablex.

Cooley, W. (1993). The difficulty of the educational task: Implications for comparing student achievement in states, school districts, and schools. *ERS Spectrum, 11*, pp. 27–31.

Copeland, K., Winsor, P., & Osborn, J. (1994). Phonemic awareness: A consideration of research and practice. In F. Lehr & J. Osborn (Eds.), *Reading, language, and literacy: Instruction for the twenty-first century* (pp. 25–44). Hillsdale, NJ: Erlbaum.

Cunningham, P. M. (1975/1976). Investigating a synthesized theory of mediated word identification. *Reading Research Quarterly, 11*, 127–143.

Dole, J. A., Duffy, G. G., Roehler, L. R., & Pearson, P. D. (1991). Moving from the old to the new: Research on reading comprehension instruction. *Review of Educational Research, 61*(2), 239–264.

Duffelmeyer, F. A., Merkley, Fyfe, & Kruse. (1994). Further validation and enhancement of the names test. *The Reading Teacher, 48*(2), 118–128.

Durkin, D. (1978–79). What classroom observations reveal about reading comprehension instruction. *Reading Research Quarterly, 14*(4), 481–533.

Durkin, D. (1986). Reading methodology textbooks: Are they helping teachers teach comprehension? *The Reading Teacher, 39*(5), 410–417.

Eastman, P. D. (1961). *Go, Dog, Go!* New York: Random House.

Education Commission of the States and The Charles A. Dana Foundation. (1996). *Bridging the gap between neuroscience and education*. Denver, CO: Author.

Ehri, L. C. (1994). Development of the ability to read words: Update. In R. B. Ruddell, M. P. Ruddell, & H. Singer (Eds.), *Theoretical models and processes of reading* (4th ed., pp. 323–358). Newark, DE: International Reading Association.

Englert, C. S., Raphael, T. E., Anderson, L. M., Anthony, H. M., & Stevens, D. D. (1991). Making strategies and self-talk visible: Writing instruction in regular and special education classrooms. *American Educational Research Journal, 28*(2), 337–372.

Fielding, L. G., & Pearson, P. D. (1994, February). Reading comprehension: What works. *Educational Leadership, 51*, 62–68.

Garner, R. (1987). *Metacognition and reading comprehension*. Norwood, NJ: Ablex.

Garnier, H. E., Stein, J. A., & Jacobs, J. K. (1997). The process of dropping out of high school: A 19-year perspective. *American Educational Research Journal, 34*(2), 395–419.

Gaskins, I.W., Downer, M., Anderson, R. C., Cunningham, P. M., Gaskins, R. W., & Schommer, M. (1988). A metacognitive approach to phonics: Using what you know to decode what you don't know. *Remedial and Special Education*, 9, 36–41, 66.

Gentile, C. (1992). *Exploring new methods for collecting students' school-based writing: NAEP's 1990 portfolio study*. Princeton, NJ: National Assessment of Educational Progress.

Goswami, U., & Bryant, P. (1990). *Phonological skills and learning to read*. East Sussex, UK: Earlbaum.

Goswami, U., & Bryant, P. (1992). Rhyming, analogy, and children's reading. In P. B. Gough, L. C. Ehri, & R. Treiman (Eds.), *Reading Acquisition* (pp. 107–143). Hillsdale, NJ: Erlbaum.

Graves, M. F. (1992). The elementary vocabulary curriculum: What should it be? In M. J. Dreher, & W. H. Slater (Eds.), *Elementary school literacy: Critical issues* (pp. 101–131). Norwood, MA: Christopher-Gordon.

Graves, M. F., Watts, S. & Graves, B. (1994). *Essentials of classroom teaching: Elementary reading methods*. Boston: Allyn and Bacon.

Graves, M. F. (1986). Vocabulary learning and instruction. In E. Z. Rothkopf (Ed.), *Review of research in education* (Vol. 13, pp. 49–90). Washington, D.C.: American Educational Research Association.

Greaney, V., & Hegarty, P. E. (1987). Correlations of leisure-time reading. *Journal of Research in Reading*, 10, 3–20.

Gunning, T. G. (1996). *Creating reading instruction for all children* (2nd ed.). Boston: Allyn and Bacon.

Hafner, A., Ingles, S., Schneider, B., & Stevenson, D. (1990). *National educational longitudinal study of 1988: A profile of the American eighth grader (NELS:88)*. (Report No. NCES= 90-458). National Center for Education Statistics, Washington, DC: Office of Educational Research and Improvement, U.S. Department of Education.

Hawley, W. D., Rosenholtz, S., Goodstein, H. J., & Hasselbring, T. (1984). School leadership and student learning. *Peabody Journal of Education*, 61(4), 53–83.

Heller, M. F. (1991). *Reading-writing connections: From theory to practice*. New York: Longman.

Hillocks, G. (1987). Synthesis of research on teaching writing. *Educational Leadership*, 44(8), 71–82.

Hoffman, J. V., Roser, N. L, & Battle, J. (1993). Reading aloud in classrooms: From the modal to a "model." *Reading Teacher*, 46(6), 496–503.

Jenkins, J. R., Stein, M. L., & Wysocki, K. (1984). Learning vocabulary through reading. *American Educational Research Journal*, 21(4), 767–787.

Johnson, D. W., & Johnson, R. T. (1989). *Cooperation and competition: Theory and research*. Edina, MN: Interaction Book Company.

Johnston, P., & Allington, R. (1991). Remediation. In P. D. Pearson, R. Barr, M. L. Kamil,& P. Mosenthal, (Eds.), *Handbook of reading research* (Vol. 2) (pp. 984–1012). White Plains, NY: Longman.

Joyce, B., & Calhoun, E. (1998). *Learning to teach inductively.* Boston: Allyn and Bacon.

Joyce, B., Weil, M. & Showers, B. (1996). *Models of teaching* (5th ed.). Boston: Allyn and Bacon.

Juel, C. (1988). Learning to read and write: A longitudinal study of fifty-four children from first through fourth grades. *Journal of Educational Psychology, 80,* 437–447.

Juel, C. (1992). Longitudinal research on learning to read and write with at-risk students. In M. J. Dreher & W. H. Slater (Eds.), *Elementary school literacy: Critical issues* (pp. 73–79). Norwood, MA: Christopher-Gordon.

Kaufman, P., McMillen, M. M., & Bradby, D. (1992). *Dropout rates in the United States: 1991.* (Report No. NCES-92-129). Washington, DC: National Center for Education Statistics, Office of Educational Research and Improvement, U.S. Department of Education.

Krashen, S. (1993). *The power of reading: Insights from the research.* Englewood, CO: Libraries Unlimited.

Langer, J. A. (1986). *Children reading and writing: Structures and strategies.* Norwood, NJ: Ablex.

Langer, J. A., Bartolome, L., Vasquez, O., & Lucas, T. (1990). Meaning construction in School literacy tasks: A study of bilingual students. *American Educational Research Journal, 27*(3), 427–471.

Levin, J. R., McCormick, C. B., Miller, G. E., Berry, J. K., & Pressley, M. (1982). Mnemonic versus Nonmnemonic vocabulary learning strategies for children. *American Educational Research Journal, 19*(1), 121–136.

Lloyd, D. N. (1978). Prediction of school failure from third-grade data. *Educational and Psychological Measurement, 38,* 1193–1200.

McGill-Franzen, A. (1994). Compensatory and special education: Is there accountability for learning and belief in children's potential? In E. H. Hiebert & B. M. Taylor (Eds.), *Getting reading right from the start: Effective early literacy interventions* (pp. 13–35). Boston: Allyn & Bacon.

Millard, E. (1997). *Differently literate: Boys, girls, and the schooling of literacy.* London: Falmer Press.

Moore, D. R., & Davenport, S. (1988). *The new improved sorting machine.* Madison: National Center on Effective Secondary Schools.

Morris, R. (1997, September). *How new research on brain development will influence educational policy.* Presentation to Policy Makers Institute, Georgia Center for Advanced Telecommunications Technology, Atlanta, GA.

Morrow, L. M., & Weinstein, C. (1986). Encouraging voluntary reading: The impact of a literature program on children's use of library centers. *Reading Research Quarterly, 21*(3), 330–346.

Moss, B. (1995). Using children's nonfiction tradebooks as read-alouds. *Language Arts, 72*(2), 122–126.

Moss, B., Leone, S. & Dipillo, M. L. (1997). Exploring the literature of fact: Linking reading and writing through information tradebooks. *Language Arts, 74*(6),

418–429.

Mullis, I. V. S., Campbell, J. R., & Farstrup, A. E. (1993). *NAEP 1992 reading report card for the nation and the states*. Princeton, NJ: Educational Testing Service.

Myers, J. (1992). The social contexts of school and personal literacy. *Reading Research Quarterly, 27*(4), 297–333.

Nagy, W. E., Anderson, R. C. (1984). How many words are there in printed school English? *Reading Research Quarterly, 19*, 304–330.

Nagy, W. E., Anderson, R. C., & Herman, P. A. (1987). Learning word meanings from context during normal reading. *American Educational Research Journal, 24*(2), 237–270.

Nagy, W. E., Herman, P. A., & Anderson, R. C. (1985). Learning words from context. *Reading Research Quarterly, 20*, 233–253.

Nagy, W. E., Winsor, P., Osborn, J., & O'Flahavan, J. (1994). Structural analysis: Some guidelines for instruction." In F. Lehr & J. Osborn (Eds.), *Reading, language, and literacy: Instruction for the twenty-first century* (pp. 45–58). Hillsdale, N.J.: Erlbaum.

Neuman, S. (1986). The home environment and fifth-grade students' leisure reading. *Elementary School Journal, 86*, 335–343.

Palinscar, A. S. (1986). The role of dialogue in providing scaffolded instruction. *Educational Psychologist, 21*(1&2), 73–98.

Pearson, P. D. (1992). Reading. In M. C. Alkin (Ed.), *Encyclopedia of Educational Research* (6th ed., Vol. 3) (pp. 1075–1085). New York: Macmillan.

Pearson, P. D., & Dole, J. A. (1987). Explicit comprehension instruction: A review of research and a new conceptualization of instruction. *Elementary School Journal, 88*(2), 151–165.

Peregoy, S. F., & Boyle, O. F. (1997). *Reading, writing, and learning in ESL*. White Plains, NY: Longman.

Pikulski, J. J. (1997). *Emergent literacy survey/K–2*. Boston: Houghton Mifflin.

Pitts, S. (1986). Read aloud to adult learners? Of course! *Reading Psychology, 7*, 35–42.

Pressley, M., Levin, J. R., & McDaniel, M. A. (1987). Remembering versus inferring what a word means: Mnemonic and contextual approaches. In M. G. McKeown & M. E. Curtis (Eds.), *The nature of vocabulary acquisition* (pp. 107–127). Hillsdale, NJ: Erlbaum.

Ramey, C. T., & Ramey, S. L. (1998, February). Early intervention and early experience. *American Psychologist, 53*(2), 109–120.

Roehler, L. R. (1991). *Embracing the instructional complexities of reading instruction*. East Lansing, MI: Institute for Research on Teaching, Michigan State University (ERIC Document Reproduction Service No. ED 340 005)

Shanahan, T. (1988, March). The reading-writing relationship: Seven instructional principles. *The Reading Teacher 41*, 636–647.

Shanahan, T. (1990). Reading and writing together: What does it really mean? In T. Shanahan (Ed.), *Reading and writing together: New perspectives for the classroom* (pp. 1–18). Norwood, MA: Christopher-Gordon.

Sharan, S. (1990). *Cooperative learning: Theory and research*. New York: Praeger.

Slavin, R. E. (1995). *Cooperative learning: Theory, research, and practice* (2nd ed.). Boston: Allyn and Bacon.

Stahl, S. A. (1999). *Vocabulary development*. Cambridge, MA: Brookline Books.

Stahl, S. A., & Fairbanks, M. M. (1986). The effects of vocabulary instruction: A model-based meta-analysis. *Review of Educational Research, 56*(1), 72–110.

Stauffer, R. G. (1969). *Directing reading maturity as a cognitive process*. New York: Harper and Row.

Sternberg, R. J. (1987). Most vocabulary is learned from context. In M. G. McKeown & and M. E. Curtis (Eds.), *The nature of vocabulary acquisition* (pp. 89–105). Hillsdale, NJ: Erlbaum.

Sternberg, R. J., & Powell, J. S. (1983). Comprehending verbal comprehension. *American Psychologist, 38*, 878–893.

Stotsky, S. (1983). Research on reading/writing relationships: A synthesis and suggested directions. *Language Arts, 60*(5), 627–642.

Tierney, R. J., & Pearson, P. D. (1985). Toward a composing model of reading. In C. N. Hedley & A. N. Baratta (Eds.), *Contexts of reading* (pp. 63–78). Norwood, NJ: Ablex.

Tierney, R. J., & Shanahan, T. (1991). Research on the reading-writing relationship: Interactions, transaction, and outcomes. In P. D. Pearson, R. Barr, M. L. Kamil,& P. Mosenthal, (Eds.), *Handbook of reading research* (Vol. 2, pp. 984–1012). White Plains, NY: Longman.

Treiman, R. (1992). The role of intrasyllabic units in learning to read. In P. Gough, L. C. Ehri, and R. Treiman (Eds.), *Reading acquisition* (pp. 65–106). Hillsdale, NJ: Erlbaum.

Wendelin, K. H., & Zinck, R. A. (1983). How students make book choices. *Reading Horizons, 23*, 84–88.

White, T., Power, M., & White, S. (1989). Morphological analysis: Implications for teaching and understanding vocabulary growth. *Reading Research Quarterly, 24*, 283–304.

Winograd, P. N., & Bridge, C. A. (1995). Teaching for literacy. In J. H. Block, S. T. Everson, & T. R. Guskey (Eds.), *School improvement programs: A handbook for educational leaders* (pp. 229–246). New York: Scholastic.

About the Author

Emily F. Calhoun directs The Phoenix Alliance, based in St. Simons Island, Georgia. A specialist in language arts and action research, she divides her time between extensive school renewal programs and research on teaching and action research.

Printed in the United States
213436BV00003B/1/A

9 780871 203373